recognizing the effects of sibling abuse

Vernon R. Wiehe, Ph.D.

WITHDRAWN
Monroe Coll. Library

SaferSocietyPress
PO Box 340
Brandon, VT 05733-0340
Phone: (802) 247-3132

HV
6626.52
Monroe Coll. Library
.W52
1996

© Copyright 1996
by Vernon Wiehe and The Safer Society Press

All rights are reserved under international and Pan-American copyright conventions. No part of this publication may be reproduced, stored in a retrieval system, or transmitted in any form or by any means, electronic, mechanical, photocopying, recording or otherwise, without the express written permission of the author or publisher, except for brief quotations in critical reviews.

Design: Holly McGovern, Whitman Communications, Inc.

Editors: Euan Bear, Alan V. Hewat

ISBN: 1-884444-21-0

Order from:
The Safer Society Press
P.O. Box 340
Brandon, VT 05733-0340

$10.00
Payable in U.S. funds only
Bulk discounts available

About the Author

Vernon R. Wiehe, Ph.D. is a professor in the College of Social Work at the University of Kentucky at Lexington. After he received a master's degree from the University of Chicago, he did postgraduate work in the Program of Advanced Studies in Social Work at Smith College. He received his Ph.D. from Washington University in St. Louis.

Dr. Wiehe is the author of many articles in professional journals as well as three previous books on sibling abuse: *Sibling Abuse, The Hidden Physical, Emotional and Sexual Trauma; Perilous Rivalry: When Siblings Become Abusive;* and *Working with Child Abuse and Neglect.* He recently co-authored (with Ann Richards) a book on acquaintance rape entitled, *Intimate Betrayal, The Trauma of Acquaintance Rape.*

Dr. Wiehe has appeared on several television and radio talk shows discussing family violence including "Donahue" and "Sonya Live." He is frequently cited as a leading researcher on the subject of family violence.

Contents

7 **Foreword**

9 **Chapter One**
A Message to the Reader

19 **Chapter Two**
Sibling Abuse —What Is It?

27 **Chapter Three**
He Hit Me: Physical Abuse

37 ***Chapter Four***
She's Picking on Me: Emotional Abuse

53 **Chapter Five**
I Can't Talk About It: Sexual Abuse

65 **Chapter Six**
When Parents Are No Help

79 **Chapter Seven**
Beyond Blame: Understanding My Parents' Response

89 **Chapter Eight**
Recognizing the Effects of Sibling Abuse in My Life

109 **Chapter Nine**
Now What? Life Choices for Sibling Abuse Survivors

121 **Reminders**

122 **Recommended Books and Videos**

124 **Select Safer Society Publications**

Foreword

This is a book about discovering and healing from a form of abuse that many adults experienced in childhood, but that few survivors—and virtually no legal or social service agencies—have ever acknowledged. Sibling abuse is the physical, emotional, and sexual abuse of one child by another child within the same family; it is largely ignored in our society. I was prompted to write this book after many victims of sibling abuse and mental health professionals working with victims in therapy requested copies of the questionnaire I had used in the research that served as the basis for my first book on this subject. They wished to use the questionnaire as a way to uncover abuse from a sibling and to begin the process of healing from the serious effects the abuse has had on their adult lives.

I want to thank the 150 people who participated in my research on sibling abuse and made this and my previous books on this subject possible. Their courage and willingness to share both the pain and suffering they experienced in childhood from a sibling and the paths to healing they have taken are an inspiration to others.

My wish for you is that your journey of uncovering the abuse you experienced from a sibling and beginning the process of healing will bring you a renewed sense of happiness and fulfillment in your life.

Vernon R. Wiehe, Ph.D.

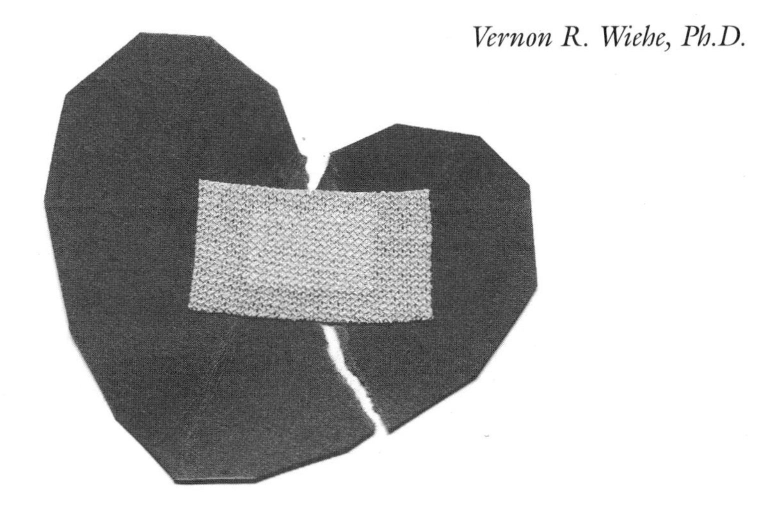

"I have tried to forget the way my older brother treated me as a child but the memories keep returning. In many ways I'm still affected as an adult by the way he treated me as a child."

Chapter One
A Message to the Reader

As you read this book, you are about to begin a journey. Just as there are various reasons for taking any journey, there are probably many reasons why you have selected this book. You might have been intrigued by the title when you saw the book at your local bookstore or public library. You might have said to yourself, "There I am. That book deals with something I've often thought about." Or perhaps, "That's interesting. I've never considered that the way some brothers and sisters treat each other might be called abuse." Most likely, however, underlying your interest in this book is a recollection of unpleasant experiences you had as a child with your brother or sister.

Perhaps even as you think about what you are now reading, unpleasant childhood memories come to mind. (Incidentally, much of what is written in this book about relationships among siblings also holds true for peers.) You may have tried to ignore these memories and the uncomfortable feelings that accompany them, but they still come to the surface of your awareness from time to time.

We often attempt to forget the traumas in our lives. Psychologists call this *suppressing* the event or experience. But our minds continue to deal with those traumas by recalling them whenever similar situations arise. In this way, the mind continues to reprocess an unpleasant event, and to associate its impact with problems we may currently be experiencing in our lives.

Someone once compared the painful memories that we try to avoid or forget, but that keep coming back, to a huge weight on our body that cannot be lifted. But *all* weights can be lifted! I have a friend who owns a moving company that specializes in moving industrial equipment, gigantic machines that you'd think would be impossible to budge once they are in place. But he does it, proving over and over that no matter how great the weight, it can be lifted—with the proper tools. A single lever placed at the right distance and the proper angle can move a tremendous weight.

So it is with painful, unpleasant, or distressing memories. Although we cannot entirely forget them, they can be defused of their destructive energy, so that the pain and suffering we feel when we recall them disappears—that is, their weight is lifted.

It's like remembering the death of a loved one, an experience everyone shares. My father died some years ago. I loved him dearly, and at the time of his death I grieved for him. Now, although I still miss him and will never forget him, I no longer cry at the thought of his passing. He is still in my memory, but, over time, his dying has been defused of the emotional energy that I once associated with it. Counselors would say that I have *worked through* my grief over my father's death.

Well-meaning friends often tell us to simply forget a painful experience. That is easier said than done. Trying to ignore or forget painful memories will not make them go away. We have to deal with them, to *work through* the memories, if we wish to rid ourselves of the painful emotions associated with them.

The Purpose of This Book

I have written this book with a definite purpose in mind: to help you deal with unpleasant experiences in your childhood that you associate with a brother or sister. So far, I have avoided a term that must be used. I have referred to *unpleasant memories* that you may associate with your brother or sister. Now it's time to say exactly what I mean.

When I say *unpleasant memories*, I am talking about the hurtful ways you were treated by your brother or sister. This treatment may have included:

- *The hitting, slapping, constant physical harassment, or even more violent behavior you experienced, involving the use of sticks, bats, knives, or guns;*
- *The names you were repeatedly called, and the ways you were ridiculed, intimidated, or made fun of, or;*
- *The sexual behavior you were forced to engage in against your will.*

What I am referring to must be called by its real name: *sibling abuse*. The purpose of this book is to help you uncover the abuse you experienced from a sibling, to confront the abuse, and to begin the journey toward healing the effects of the abuse on your life.

Your initial reaction to reading the words *sibling abuse* may be, "Abuse? I wasn't abused: all brothers and sisters fight." You may at first want to deny that what you experienced was abuse. This is not unusual, and we will discuss it in future chapters. For example, it's possible that as a child you were overweight, so you excuse the actions of your brothers or sisters by saying that they were only trying to help you lose weight when they called you "fatso," "lardass," "tubbo," or whatever ugly names they repeatedly used. But even if their intentions were good, it doesn't erase the pain these names caused you at the time, or change the painful memories you may still feel. And even if you were fat, it doesn't give anyone the liberty to abuse you.

Let's use another example. Perhaps you were forced to engage in sexual play with an older sibling. As you recall these events, you may experience shame and disgust with yourself. Perhaps the words of the sibling who forced you into these behaviors still ring in your memory: "You enjoyed it," or, "You could have stopped if you'd wanted to." You might be blaming yourself for what occurred, as many sexual abuse survivors do. *The sexual abuse is not your fault!* We will talk more about dealing with self-blame in later chapters.

Let's go back to the purpose of this book—to help you uncover and confront the abuse you experienced from a sibling when you were growing up, and begin on the path toward healing the effects of abuse on your life. Unfortunately for you, and for many other adults, for a long time sibling abuse was excused as merely sibling *rivalry*. Research, however, presents evidence to the contrary.

In the 1970s, a very important study of violence in American families took place[1] involving more than two thousand families. In this study, family members were asked to identify violent acts that had occurred in their family during the previous year. The results indicated that violent acts between siblings occurred far more frequently than violence between spouses or between parents and children. The results of this research were published in the book *Behind Closed Doors.* In 1980, when the book was published, family violence took place behind closed doors, and what went on behind the closed doors of a family's residence was regarded as no one else's business. Yet violence between spouses (spouse abuse) and violence by parents toward children (child abuse) were occurring in many American families.

In the years since *Behind Closed Doors* was published, spouse abuse and child abuse have, fortunately, received considerable attention, but sibling abuse continues to be largely ignored or overlooked. We must not ignore, however, the research finding mentioned earlier, that violent acts between siblings take place far more frequently than either spouse or child abuse.

In 1990, I published *Sibling Abuse: Hidden Physical, Emotional, and Sexual Trauma*,[2] reporting the findings of my research involving 150 adults who were survivors of sibling abuse. Because this book was primarily aimed at professionals working in the field of family violence, it was later rewritten for parents, and was published in 1991 under the title, *Perilous Rivalry: When Siblings Become Abusive.*[3]

As a result of these books, during the past several years I have been a guest on "Donahue," "Sonya Live," and many radio and television talk shows throughout the United States. The public's response to the subject of sibling abuse has been overwhelming. The telephone lines of call-in shows immediately become active, as listeners call to discuss abuse they suffered at the hands of a sibling when they were children, abuse that in some instances has continued even into their adult lives. Also, parents call to talk about their concerns regarding the fighting and name-calling their children engage in, and whether that constitutes sibling abuse.

Why the intense interest in this subject? I think it is due to the fact that sibling abuse is so common. Many individuals have spoken and written to me to say how helpful my books have been in confirming for them that what they experienced from a sibling was not *sibling rivalry* but rather sibling *abuse.* In many cases, the parents of these victims ignored or excused it as "normal sibling rivalry," "just part of growing up," or "boys will be boys."

When they hear from another source about sibling abuse, many people realize that they personally have experienced this problem. They become aware that the childhood abuse they suffered at the hands of a sibling has profoundly affected their lives as adults. Learning that they are not alone, that others have experienced this type of abuse, gives them the courage to seek help for the problems-in-living they are experiencing as adults.

In light of what has been happening recently in the field of family violence, I would also like to state what the purpose of this book is *not*: ***The purpose of this book is not to persuade or convince you that you were abused as a child by a sibling.*** This book *is* about identifying and naming what happened, sorting out what is normal conflict and what is abuse. In later chapters, you will be asked to recall the facts surrounding what happened to you. These facts will speak for themselves, and will help you decide for yourself whether what you experienced should in fact be called sibling abuse.

I have received many deeply touching letters and phone calls from survivors of sibling abuse, thanking me for bringing this subject out into the open. One reader wrote:

> If only my parents had been aware of what you are discussing in your book, my childhood might not have been the horrible experience that it was.

Below, you will find two of the many letters I have received. I share these letters with you so that you may compare your own reactions to what happened to you as a child with the reactions of others, and thus may begin to gain awareness that you are not alone in your experiences suffered at the hands of a sibling.

Dear Dr. Wiehe,

I have just read your book, *Sibling Abuse*, and had to write and say thank you for writing it. I am 27 years old and have been waiting for 20 years for someone, anyone, to acknowledge that it exists! Parents, friends, school counselors and nurses didn't believe me because "these things just don't happen." I used to fantasize about going on the Phil Donahue Show to talk about it just so people would see that it DOES happen.

When I saw your book on the shelf in the bookstore, my immediate reaction was, "Oh my God!" Next came, "It's about time." I was nervous reading it, but also felt a profound sense of relief. You see, for all that we hear about child abuse and sexual abuse, I'd never heard of anyone else being abused by a brother, as in my case. Not even in therapy or therapy groups. Growing up I always felt different and even now feel that—a sense that I can't even be abused normally!

I felt that many of the statements in the book could have been made by me. Maybe I'll have the nerve someday to send copies to my parents who still don't believe me, don't remember anything about the abuse, and wonder why I don't speak with my brother. After all, "it was so long ago and was never that bad anyway."

Few people can understand the double effect of the abuse and the failure to be validated in one's feelings and reactions. I have been made to feel that I am to blame for the results that the abuse has had on my life because people think it didn't really happen. With your book I feel validated. So, once again, thank you.

Sincerely,
(Name Withheld)

Dear Dr. Wiehe,

After 10 years of extensive abuse from my older brother and four years in mental institutions—all because of my so called frequent suicide attempts (my brother just loved knives. I still have a one-half inch scar ear to ear on my neck because I refused intercourse)—I can finally say to myself that I am not alone. Your book, *Perilous Rivalry*, is a wonderful book. I finally have written proof that sibling abuse does happen. Maybe now my family will finally believe that I *did not* try to kill myself over 50 times and finally put the blame on its rightful owner, my brother.

Sincerely,

(Name Withheld)

Your Journey

And now the journey through this book, along this path, is yours. Although we generally have a destination in mind when we take a journey, there is often an element of mystery in the experience. We never know what side trips we might take, if we are adventurous enough to leave the main highway, or what interesting experiences we might have. Some may not even be pleasant. We might be stranded with a flat tire or engine trouble. We can never anticipate everything that will happen to us on a journey, and often the unexpected events are the ones we recall most vividly afterwards. And so the journey you are beginning with the reading of this book may carry with it unexpected benefits as well as some pain, as you recall unpleasant memories of your relationship with a brother or sister when you were a child.

Just as a map serves as a guide for any journey, and suggests alternate routes and possible side trips, so the chapters of this book will serve as a guide for you on your journey toward uncovering the abuse you may have experienced from a sibling. That is the destination or goal of our journey. If you are feeling weighted down with painful memories I hope that reading this book will serve as the lever (to use an earlier analogy) that begins the process of lifting the weight of traumatic memories from you.

The journey toward uncovering the abuse includes:

- *becoming aware of the type of abuse you experienced;*
- *attempting to understand how the abuse occurred;*
- *assessing the impact the abuse has had on your life; and,*
- *seeking healing for the effects of the abuse.*

Terms to Understand

Before we begin our journey, a few terms should be defined. The sibling—a brother or sister—who engaged in the abusive behavior toward you will be referred to in the chapters that follow as the *perpetrator*. Although I refer to the perpetrator as if only one sibling engaged in the abusive behavior, in many instances victims have experienced abuse from more than one sibling. My research on sibling abuse revealed that, while often the perpetrator was an older brother or sister, at times other siblings joined in the abusive behavior, including even younger siblings who were following the example of an older brother or sister.The individual who was the object of the abusive behavior—namely, you—is generally referred to as the *victim*. However, anyone who has survived any type of abuse from another person usually does not like to be called a victim, a name that implies someone who is helpless.

Many victims of abuse have survived the abusive behavior and are struggling with its effect on their lives. Thus, they prefer to be called *survivors,* a name that implies someone who, despite a trauma or tragedy, is alive and has moved on with life, and is coping with the devastating effects of the event. So it is with survivors of sibling abuse—including you, if you experienced such abuse from a sibling. Despite what may have happened to you, you are a survivor. In the pages that follow, then, I will refer to the person to whom the abuse is occurring as a victim while it is going on, but later, when the same individual is engaged in coping with the effects of the abuse, or is involved in the healing process, I will identify that person as a survivor.

A Task for You

At the end of each chapter, there are tasks or exercises that will help you think about your childhood experiences and identify any that might be considered abusive. These exercises appear under the heading, "A Task for You." If you have been abused by a sibling, I hope that, while you read each chapter, you will be able to see something of yourself in the comments of the survivors, as they describe their own abuse at the hands of a sibling and the impact it has had on their lives. When you've finished a chapter, I would like to encourage you to sit in a comfortable chair and read the task, then close your eyes and think back on your own childhood. After a few minutes, write down your thoughts in a separate notebook. Don't worry about writing in complete sentences, but let your thoughts flow freely. Go ahead and jot down phrases that come to mind in response to the questions.

Remember, you are performing these tasks for *your own* benefit. You are not writing an essay for a teacher to read and grade. You might wish to do the tasks when you are alone, and to keep your notebook in a place where no one else will find it. Use the questions at each chapter's end to prompt your thoughts and guide you on your journey of uncovering your abuse by a sibling. If you are seeing a therapist, you might discuss what you've discovered in your counseling sessions.

After you have completed the task at the end of each chapter, additional thoughts may come to mind about the questions you answered at the end of an earlier chapter. Feel free to go back and add those thoughts to what you wrote then. This is *your* journey. Use it to the fullest extent possible *for yourself.*

If you *own* this book, you might want to highlight the passages that have special meaning for you to help you find the passages you want to reread. If you *borrowed* this book, you might want to keep a pen or pencil handy, and write in your notebook the numbers of the pages you think you will want to reread or refer to later.

Are you ready to get started? Let's begin the journey in the next chapter by answering the question: What is sibling abuse?

Endnotes

1 M. Straus, R. Gelles, & S. Steinmetz, *Behind Closed Doors* (Garden City, NJ: Anchor Books, 1980).

2 V. Wiehe, *Sibling Abuse: Hidden Physical, Emotional, and Sexual Trauma* (Lexington, MA: Lexington Books, 1990).

3 V. Wiehe, *Perilous Rivalry: When Siblings Become Abusive* (Lexington, MA: Lexington Books, 1991).

"My parents jokingly referred to the way my brother treated me as sibling rivalry. I would call it sibling abuse. They had no idea how I was suffering."

Chapter 2
Sibling Abuse – What Is It?

A**s you think back upon** your childhood, you may have distressing, unpleasant, or painful memories of experiences with a brother or sister. Some of these memories may be vague; others might be very clear. In this chapter you will begin to sort through these memories and to put some labels or some names on what occurred. By sorting and labeling your experiences you will be better able to understand what happened. Understanding will ultimately help you more effectively cope with the impact these events may have had on your life.

Was It Abuse?

First, we must look at the label we give these painful memories of the way a brother or sister treated us as we were growing up. In the previous chapter I suggested these distressing memories may have been about sibling abuse. You are probably asking yourself, "Is what happened to me sibling abuse or normal sibling rivalry?" All brothers and sisters do fight, all brothers and sisters do call each other names, and some siblings do "play doctor" or some other exploratory game that often involves some sexual contact. We've all been involved in fighting and name-calling with our siblings and probably there were times when we initiated these behaviors.

Sibling abuse, however, refers to incidents that we cannot erase from our memories. In general, these events occurred repeatedly, perhaps slightly differently each time. These occurrences remain in our memories because, as mental health professionals say, they are *emotionally charged events*: they are surrounded by feelings that don't seem to want to go away.

Here are four questions that will help you determine if the painful or upsetting memories you have about behaviors you experienced from a brother or sister should be labeled abuse. Incidentally, name calling, derogatory remarks, and repeatedly being made fun of are all included in the term *behavior*.

Question 1:
Was I repeatedly a victim of my brother(s) or sister(s)?

A victim is someone who needs help to cope with an experience that is overwhelming. For example, a victim in an automobile accident may be trapped in the car or may be unconscious, helpless and needing to be rescued. Victims often try to help themselves but they are prevented by circumstances from escaping or relieving their victimization. You may have attempted to defend yourself from the punches and slaps or tried to ignore the insults, but no matter what you did, you couldn't stop the behaviors. The abuse continued. You were a victim of your sibling.

Although occasional hitting or degrading comments may not qualify as abusive behavior, *any* sexually assaultive behavior is considered abuse, even if it happens only once. Some sexual experiences in childhood are normal. "I'll show you mine if you'll show me yours" might be normal exploration, curiosity about bodies in preschool children. Sometimes this activity takes the form of "playing doctor." If the situation was mutual, meaning that both children had an equal right and power to say "No, I don't want to," if it was fun and not scary, then it probably was not abusive.

Question 2:
How frequently and how long did the behavior occur?

We can all remember hearing angry words from a sibling or exchanging punches or slaps when we were involved in a fight with a brother or sister. These are part of normal sibling interactions and we refer to these behaviors as sibling rivalry. But when they occur repeatedly and over a long period of time, they cross the line into *sibling abuse*. Generally, except for certain sexual behaviors, events that happen only once do not become emotionally charged. We might remember them, but we no longer feel the emotional pain associated with their occurrence because they did not persist.

Question 3:
Was the behavior age-appropriate?

Let's apply a few examples to this question. A two-year-old and a four-year-old struggle over some toys, and one child ends up crying because the other takes away his favorite plaything. Is their struggle appropriate to their age? Yes it is. The two-year-old is probably mimicking what its older sibling is doing in play. Whichever toy the older child plays with is the toy the younger one wants.

Let's take another example. Beth is fourteen; her sister Emily is sixteen. The two siblings seem to fight continuously over privileges. Emily is allowed to date, but Beth can only go on group dates to chaperoned activities. Also, Beth has an earlier curfew than her sister, and Beth is very unhappy about it. Their bickering with each other and their parents over what Beth feels is unfair treatment is typical of two adolescents, and may appropriately be referred to as sibling rivalry.Let's take this example a bit further. Beth is frequently angry at her parents for not giving her the same privileges as her older sister. She takes her anger out on Emily with name-calling. She constantly refers to her sister as "Butt-head." She delights in embarrassing Emily in front of friends at school by calling her this name, and when Emily's dates come to their home, Beth continually refers to her sister as "Butt-head" in their presence. Emily has asked her sister to stop this name-calling, but Beth won't give it up. It's not unusual behavior to call a sibling a name, but to persist in this activity, and to repeatedly and knowingly embarrass a sibling in front of others, takes the behavior beyond the range of normal sibling rivalry and into the area of sibling abuse.

Let's look at one final example. Two siblings, a brother and sister three and four years old, are taking a bath together. The older sibling notices that her brother's genitals are different from hers. She touches his penis. Is this sibling abuse? No, because this is not unusual behavior, it is not coercive (there is nothing indicating that either child was forced or threatened), and it is age-appropriate. Their parents should take this as a cue to begin to explain to the children that boys and girls have different genitals, and to share with them the difference between good and secret touches, including the lesson to say "No" to secret touches.

Now let's change this example. Tommy is thirteen years old; his sister is five. Tommy takes his five-year-old sister into his tree house, makes her take off her clothes, and fondles her genitals. This behavior is inappropriate for a thirteen-year-old boy. By this age, he should have received enough sex education to understand the differences between boys and girls, and the difference between good touches and secret touches. What Tommy is engaging in with his younger sister is abusive behavior.

Question 4:
What is the purpose of the behavior?

This final question to help you separate normal sibling rivalry from sibling abuse focuses on why a sibling was engaging in the behavior.

Let's look again at some of the previous examples. The two small children taking interest in each other's genitals are primarily engaged in observation, although they should soon receive information appropriate to their ages regarding sexual differences and good and secret touches. On the other hand, when thirteen-year-old Tommy takes his five-year-old sister to his tree house and examines her genitals, he is involved in more than just observation. This young adolescent is seeking some degree of sexual pleasure at his sister's expense, which makes his behavior abusive. Finally, Beth's name-calling is clearly intended to hurt and belittle her sister Emily in front of Emily's friends, and is purposely destructive behavior. It is an inappropriate way for Beth to express her anger and resolve the conflicts she feels with her sister and their parents. A more appropriate approach would be for the sisters to try some supervised problem-solving, assisted by their parents.

Types of Sibling Abuse

We have discussed ways to distinguish between behaviors that may be considered normal sibling rivalry and those that can be labeled sibling abuse. Now let's look at the different types of abusive sibling behavior. Three categories of abuse will be discussed: physical, emotional, and sexual.

Physical abuse.

This type of abuse consists of willful acts by a sibling that result in pain or physical injury. It includes pinching, pushing, tying up, playing violent games, hitting, biting, kicking, terrorizing, or even more violent behavior involving instruments such as sticks, bats, knives or guns.

Emotional abuse.

This type of abuse is also known as *psychological maltreatment*. Our parents might have referred to some forms of emotional abuse as "teasing," though most people think of teasing as essentially light-hearted and not meant maliciously. "Teasing" is a catch-all word that covers a number of behaviors, including abusive behaviors designed to belittle, ridicule, intimidate, annoy, provoke, and harass. In accounts of sibling abuse survivors, other behaviors, such as the deliberate destruction of personal property or pets, go well beyond "teasing" and fall within the category of emotional abuse. Emotional abuse among siblings has a more serious impact than is immediately apparent. Researchers in the field of child abuse regard emotional abuse as the most wide-spread and potentially the most destructive form of abuse.[4] Emotional abuse often underlies and accompanies physical and sexual abuse. It rarely comes to the attention of the courts, largely because it leaves no tangible evidence. No wounds, marks, or bruises can be seen as a result of emotional abuse. The "wounds" are inside the victim's mind and spirit, affecting the victim's sense of self-esteem and self-worth. The harmful effects of emotional abuse are even worse when parents fail to recognize or acknowledge it, when they excuse it as normal behavior, or, worst of all, when they join in.

Sexual abuse.

This type of abuse can involve physical contact or not involve touch at all. Forms of contact sexual abuse include one sibling's sexually touching another or asking the other to sexually touch him or her, attempted penetration, intercourse, and sodomy. Non-contact or non-touch sexual abuse can include unwanted sexual references in conversation, indecent exposure, forcing a sibling to observe the sexual behaviors of another (such as masturbation), taking pornographic pictures, or forcing a sibling to look at pornographic materials.

Although sexual abuse (whether among siblings or other family members, or committed by strangers) is a problem society would prefer to ignore, there are statistics that show how serious and widespread this problem is. If you are the victim of sibling sexual abuse, this information will help you see that you are not alone in your victimization.

- A survey of 796 undergraduates at six New England colleges found that 15 percent of the females and 10 percent of the males reported having had some kind of sexual experience involving a sibling.
  - Fondling and touching genitals were the most common activities reported in all age categories.
  - 25 percent of the incidents could be regarded as exploitive, because force was used and because of the considerable age differences between those involved.
  - 40 percent of the students reported that they were younger than eight years old when the sexual experiences took place. In 73 percent of the incidents, at least one of the participants was older than eight, and in 35 percent one of the participants was older than twelve.[5]

- In a sample of 930 women residents of San Francisco who were eighteen and over, a researcher found that 16 percent (150 women) reported having suffered at least one experience of sexual abuse with a family member—parent, uncle, grandparent, or sibling—before the age of eighteen. These women reported a total of 187 sexual episodes with different related perpetrators.
  - 31 percent of the sample reported having been abused by a nonrelative before they turned eighteen.
  - Altogether, 38 percent (353) of the women surveyed had been sexually abused by perpetrators from inside or outside their families before they were eighteen, and 28 percent (260) reported at least one such experience before age fourteen.[6]

These studies probably underestimate the incidence of sibling sexual abuse because, as might be the case in your own experience, feelings of embarrassment and shame may have kept the victims from reporting the abuse to their parents or any other adults. Also, like other victims of sexual abuse, they were likely to have unfairly blamed themselves for what happened. Thus, the number of incidents of sexual abuse disclosed by these studies, like the accounts of survivors who will speak in subsequent chapters, represent only the tip of the iceberg of sibling sexual abuse.

A Task for You

Before we hear from some survivors of sibling abuse in the next few chapters, please complete this task. This exercise will help you recall the structure of your family when you were a child, the number of your siblings and your relationship in age to each of them.

In a separate notebook, write the title of this task at the top of the page: *My Family as I was Growing Up.* Identify your family members by making a list. On the first two lines, please write the names of your parents and their relationship to you (Mother, Father, Stepfather, and so on). If one of your parents had died, or you had a step-parent, or lived with your grandparents, or your parent had a live-in partner, change the title "Mother" or "Father" to show who is who. Also, if you had more than one father or mother during your childhood because of divorce, desertion, or death, please include this information.

After you have identified your parents, list all the children (each on a separate line), from the oldest to the youngest, and include yourself. Identify the difference in your ages with a plus or minus sign and the number of years. For example, if you had two older brothers, Tom, six years older than you, and Dale, four years older, and a sister, Mary, three years younger than you, your list of siblings should look like this:

Example:

Siblings:	*age*
Tom	+6
Dale	+4
Myself	—
Mary	–3

Endnotes

[4] S. Hart & M. Brassard, "A major threat to children's mental health—psychological maltreatment," *American Psychologist* 42 (1987): 160-165.

[5] D. Finkelhor, "Sex among siblings: A survey of prevalence, variety, and effects," *Archives of Sexual Behavior 9* (1980): 171-193.

[6] D. Russell, *The Secret Trauma: Incest in the Lives of Girls and Women* (New York: Basic Books, 1986).

"As I look back on my childhood, I seem to have spent so much time protecting myself from my older brother who was constantly hitting me. He made my life miserable!"

Chapter 3
He Hit Me: Physical Abuse

We have talked about three types of sibling abuse—physical, emotional, and sexual. In the next several chapters, we are going to hear from survivors of each of these types of abuse, who will tell about their experiences. In this chapter, they will describe the physical abuse they suffered from siblings.

Three forms of sibling physical abuse have been identified in the survivors' accounts that follow:

1) The most common forms—hitting, biting, slapping, shoving, and punching;
2) An unusual form—tickling;
3) Injurious or life-threatening forms—for example, smothering, choking, shooting with a BB gun.

As you read these stories from survivors, think about your own experiences with your brother(s) and/or sister(s).

The Most Common Forms

Abuse survivors report that the most common forms of physical victimization they suffered at the hands of siblings involved slapping, pushing, punching, biting, hair pulling, scratching, and pinching. Some survivors remember having been hit with objects—including rubber hoses, coat hangers, hairbrushes, belts, and sticks—and threatened or stabbed with broken glass, knives, razor blades, and scissors.

Remember our discussion in the previous chapter about distinguishing between sibling *abuse* and sibling *rivalry*. What you are going to hear from survivors in the following pages are not reports of single incidents but accounts of childhoods marked by frequent acts of physical aggression or abuse. The *repeated pattern* of these acts is what defines the behavior as sibling *abuse* rather than sibling rivalry.

A 40-year-old woman from Kentucky recalls the abuse she received from two older brothers:

> *My brothers typically slugged me in the arm. I was not to cry or everyone went to their rooms. The other favorite activity was to play scissors, paper, and stone. My wrist would be stinging from the hits when I lost. My older brother would usually hit me in the stomach, push me down on the floor, and hold me down while he continued to hit me in the stomach and on the arms.*

A New Mexico woman describes the abuse she suffered from her brother:

> *He would engage me in wrestling matches daily, typically punching me in the stomach until I could not breathe, torturing my joints—wrists, knees, and fingers—spitting on me, putting his knees on my arms, and pinning me down and beating on my chest with his knuckles.*

A 42-year-old woman from Wisconsin vividly remembers abuse inflicted by older siblings:

> *I remember frequently being curled up in a living room chair with my hands over my face being hit over and over. I usually ended up on the floor not moving or making noises so they would go away.*

An adult survivor who was handicapped as a child has shared a sad history of physical abuse by her older brother:

> *As early as I can recall, I remember my brother hitting me, playing nasty tricks on me to hurt me, hitting me even worse if I told my parents on him. I was crippled from osteomyelitis and polio but this made no difference to him, except perhaps to make me the perfect victim. My brother would tie a rope across the walking space between a chest of drawers and the bed. He would call me to come. When I came he would pull the rope and trip me. I lived in constant fear of him.*

A survivor from Kansas describes the physical abuse she went through, and provides insight into her brother's motivation:

> *He would start by taking jabs at my face and force me into a corner or until I fell over something and was down. Then he would pound at my shoulders until I cried or pleaded for him to stop, usually telling him I would do his work for him.*

An Illinois survivor describes a similar situation:

> *A verbal fight would start and he would punch me with closed fists in the arms or back. Usually this occurred around issues of him dominating me. He would resort to physical abuse so he could dominate me.*

Similarly, another respondent writes:

Through high school, my brother would twist my arms or pin me down and bend my arms or legs to get me to agree to do things he wanted me to do, such as his chores or to cover for him by lying to my parents. If I told my parents, my brother would say I was lying and then we would both get punished.

If the parents did not intervene, the perpetrator soon realized that he or she could gain absolute control over a sibling through physical abuse. The older or stronger siblings had the power to force the younger ones to do whatever they—the older ones—wanted, and their abusive actions left their victims powerless.

A Canadian survivor attests to how helpless younger siblings are in such a situation:

> *My brother was very strong. He would hold my arms down with his knees and slap me or tickle me. Also, he would grab my hands and make me slap myself. He would punch me a lot, but not in the face or anywhere you could see obvious bruises. I was powerless to resist.*

Although most of the perpetrators referred to have been brothers, some survivors talked about the abuse they experienced from sisters.

This adult survivor of sibling physical abuse provides an example:

> *My sister would hit, kick, or spit at me. Although she was only one year older, she was always much stronger and bigger than me.*

An Unusual Form—Tickling

Perhaps you never thought of tickling as abusive, but many survivors have described it as a form of physical abuse. Not the harmless tickling that almost everyone has engaged in at one time or another with a brother or sister. To qualify as abuse, it must be *relentless* tickling, which the perpetrators will not stop despite the victims' pleas for them to do so. The fact that siblings often tickle each other in harmless play may explain why parents frequently overlook the seriousness of this behavior when it turns harmful.

We all know that sometimes, in a context of mutual respect and trust, tickling can be pleasant. At such times, the victim is confident that the perpetrator will stop when asked. But tickling can also be painful. The unpleasantness often associated with tickling is due to the fact that the nerve fibers that respond to tickling are the same ones that respond to pain.When a victim asks that the tickling be stopped but the perpetrator continues, the behavior begins to become abusive. Tickling becomes an expression of hostility and power. As you will read in the following comments, perpetrators often ignored their victims' pleading until the victims vomited or wet their pants. Frequently, the perpetrators pinned their victims to the floor, or held their arms behind their backs.

A survivor from Missouri writes:

> *My brother and sister would hold me down and tickle me until I cried. They considered this play and would usually do it when our parents were gone. Often I would be in tears. They would finally let me go and then laugh because I was a "crybaby."*

A 48-year-old woman from Minnesota reports:

> *I was unmercifully tickled by my brother, who held down every limb and body part that wiggled and covered my mouth when I cried and yelled for help. He pulled my hair after I pulled his, thinking that would hurt him and he would stop.*

Here an older sister relentlessly tickled a younger sibling:

> *My older sister who was much stronger than me would begin by punching, slapping, and eventually pinning me to the floor. After pinning me to the floor, she would tickle me to the point that I would vomit.*

Injurious or Life-Threatening Physical Abuse

Small injuries often occur when brothers and sisters play, especially if an argument develops and feelings slip out of control. Even larger injuries, broken bones for example, may happen accidentally in rough sports. But the injurious or life-threatening behaviors described by these survivors below are not simple, isolated incidents of ordinary childhood. Unfortunately, they are typical of the way some siblings, usually older and larger, treat their younger or smaller brothers or sisters.

In many instances, the accounts that follow might best be understood in light of the parents' reactions. Usually, when a child is injured by a brother or sister while they play together, parents will comfort the hurt child, see to his or her injuries, and discipline the sibling who caused the harm. Most importantly, the parents will attempt to find out what happened, so that it does not occur again. However, when parents react to a child's being injured by a brother or sister with a "don't-care attitude," tell the child to quit crying, act as if nothing happened, or even blame the child for his or her own injuries, the incident becomes abusive.

A 55-year-old woman describes two injurious events that produced scars which still remind her of her sister's abusive behavior:

> *I climbed on the chicken coop and a nail penetrated my foot. It went all the way through my foot. I was literally nailed to the coop. My older sister saw me and laughed and told me that's what I deserved. She left and wouldn't help me down. After a long time my older brother came by, helped me get down, and took me to the hospital for a tetanus shot. I was so afraid I would get lockjaw. I still have the scar on my foot. Once my sister was ironing. She was a teen-ager; I was between four and five. I was curious as to what she was doing. I put my hands flat up on the ironing board and she immediately put the hot iron down on my hand. She laughed and told me to get lost. I still have the burn scar on my left hand.*

Another survivor of severe physical abuse writes:

> *My young brother would chase me with a BB gun and shoot at my feet and legs. He liked to see me "dance," as he called it. I was always afraid to be around him when he was playing with his BB gun because you were not safe.*

A frightening account of life-threatening physical abuse by an older brother comes from this California survivor:

> *My brother discovered that hitting me in the stomach would cause me to black out. So, he used to hit me there and watch me pass out.*

A woman from Texas, who describes herself as being extremely afraid of people, especially men, also experienced abuse from an older brother:

> *My oldest brother would put his arms around my chest tight and not let me inhale any air while I had to watch in the mirror as he laughed and explained how I was going to die.*

Similarly, another survivor recalls a brother's life-threatening abuse:

> *Under the guise of "play-fighting," my older brother would choke me until I*

was gagging. As he got older and stronger, this got more vicious.

Several respondents reported that their siblings had smothered them with pillows, usually when a fight developed between brothers and sisters playing together on a couch or bed. Once siblings discovered the power and control they could gain through the use of a pillow, this behavior would be repeated.

Three survivors related their terrifying experiences of being nearly smothered:

I remember my brother putting a pillow over my head. He would hold it and laugh while I struggled to get out from under him and the pillow. I remember being terrified. I honestly thought he would smother me to death. This occurred frequently.

My brother, four years older than me, liked to put a pillow over my face. He was twice my size and very big. One time I did pass out, and I came to when he gave me mouth-to-mouth resuscitation.

My brother forced me to the bottom of my sleeping bag and held the top closed so I couldn't get out or breathe. When I realized I couldn't get out, I became panic-stricken and thought I was going to die. Even as I write this, I am taken back to that moment and feel just the way I felt then. As an adult, I'm claustrophobic and can't have my face covered without panic setting in.

A sibling abuse victim from Louisiana, the youngest of four children, describes another form of injurious or life-threatening abuse:

I don't remember when it started, but my brothers and sisters used to hit me in the stomach to knock the breath out of me because I had asthma and they thought it was funny to see me wheeze. I was around four or five years of age. Also, my brothers and sisters would hit me in the nose to make me sneeze and count the number of times I would sneeze. Whoever made me sneeze the most was the winner. Once I sneezed seventeen times. On another occasion I bled from my nose all over a new chair my parents had bought after my brother hit me in the nose.

Drowning, yet another form of injurious or life-threatening physical abuse inflicted by siblings, is recalled in these painful testimonies:

My brother made several serious attempts to drown me in local pools and later laughed about it. These attempts continued until I was strong enough to get away and could swim.

I was three or four years old. My family went camping often. We were out at a little lake. I was walking with my two older brothers. We walked out on a dock to see the ducks, and my brother pushed me into the water. I couldn't swim! They just stood on the dock and laughed at me. I was gasping for air. I thought I was going to die! Then the next thing I remember is someone pulling me out. It was a farmer driving by on his tractor. He took us all back to the camp, and he told my parents he had pulled me out of the water. I told my parents that my brothers had pushed me, and they said I fell in.

Regardless of the form it takes, physical abuse can assume a pattern that governs the way one sibling relates to another, especially if a parent does not intervene.

A survivor from Maine recalls:

I can't ever remember not being abused by my brother. I can't describe the first memory because he beat on me every day. It was just part of existing to me.

"Making a Mountain Out of a Molehill"?

When I was the guest on a local radio talk show, several adult women called in and described the physical abuse they had suffered at the hands of siblings when they were growing up. One told of constant beatings inflicted by an older brother, another told of two occasions when an older sister tried to drown her, and other callers reported similar situations. All of the callers said that as adults they have little contact with their abusive siblings.

Toward the end of the program a woman who was one of seven children in her family told the audience:

We fought like cats and dogs. We had bruises and scratches on our bodies all the time from the fights we had. As adults now we are very close to each other. We have get-togethers at holidays and frequently have family reunions. I think all this talk about abuse is silly. People should just forget what happened to them and quit whining. They're just making a mountain out of a molehill.

What do you think? Based on her own response to what her siblings did, it is possible that what happened to her would not qualify as *abuse*. But even though *she* later reacted positively to her shared childhood experiences with her siblings, it doesn't mean that all of her siblings felt the same way. Finally, ignoring or minimizing problems will not make them go away. The weight or effect of a problem will not remove itself—the problem must be confronted.

Telling adults who are dealing with problems-in-living because of the abuse they suffered in childhood that they should "just snap out of it" is cruel. That is not to suggest that all of us make ourselves the victims of everything that has happened in our lives. But let's be realistic and "call a spade a spade." There comes a time when we must recognize a problem and deal with it. That is what I hope this book will help you do.

Summary

The constant physical abuse that some brothers or sisters inflict makes for a very confusing climate in a child's home: is this what family love is supposed to feel like?

An Arizona survivor clearly feels this confusion:

> *As a child my parents allowed my brothers and sisters to beat me up. I was so confused as a result. I thought individuals in families were supposed to love each other, not hurt one another.*

A home climate where physical abuse is tolerated teaches a child that behaviors such as hitting, slapping, pushing, etc. are appropriate ways to solve problems. The victim also receives the message, "You deserve to be treated like this." This message has a profound effect on a child's self-esteem, and can survive into adulthood, until the child, now grown, learns that he or she did not deserve such treatment after all.

Therapy is an excellent way to change this kind of negative message. Unfortunately, not all sibling abuse survivors seek therapy, in part because no one has ever let them know that sibling abuse is a major problem. As a result, they carry the weight of these horrible life lessons around with them for a

lifetime. Later on, you can read how survivors describe problems created in their adult lives by the abusive behavior they experienced as children.

A Task for You

Now it is time for you to think about your own childhood experiences with your sibling or siblings. Think back to the time when you were growing up at home. Go back as far as you can remember—back to your days in grade school or even before, if you can remember, and on through junior high and high school. Looking at some pictures of yourself as a child in a family photo album or a school yearbook might help you remember more clearly.

Let the following questions guide you as you think back. Jot down your thoughts on a fresh page in your notebook or journal. Describe any incidents you recall. Don't worry about how you phrase it or whether the grammar or punctuation are correct. Just let your thoughts and feelings flow as you describe any pleasant or painful interactions you may have experienced with a brother or sister.

1) What are the *pleasant* memories that I have from my childhood concerning my interactions with my brothers and sisters? List them using a few words or a phrase for each.

2) What *unpleasant* or *painful* memories do I have from my childhood concerning my interactions with my brothers and sisters? List them using a few words or a phrase for each.

3) Are these unpleasant memories associated with physical behaviors like hitting, slapping, shoving, or even more serious or injurious behaviors? If so, briefly list some that you remember.

4) How often did these behaviors occur? less than once a week? at least once a week? several times a week? daily? several times a day?

5) As you recall these behaviors, try to imagine what purpose they served. Write down what you think your sibling was trying to accomplish by behaving this way toward you.

"My older sister called me 'Fatso' when I was growing up. She would do it in front of my friends and everyone. My parents never told her not to. I think they thought it would make me lose weight. It only destroyed my self-esteem. I still don't feel good about myself and I'm not fat."

Chapter 4
She's Picking on Me: Emotional Abuse

An old schoolyard saying goes, "Sticks and stones may break my bones, but words will never hurt me." While its source is unknown, this saying has been passed down through generations as a statement of truth. Although its message is that verbal attacks do no harm, you will see from the testimony of survivors of emotional abuse by siblings, or as you may know from your own personal experience, nothing could be further from the truth.

The Nature of Emotional Abuse

Emotional abuse is difficult to identify. No accepted legal standards exist, either to prove that emotional or behavioral problems result from emotional abuse or to determine the seriousness of this type of abuse. Nor does emotional abuse leave physical evidence, such as abrasions, wounds, blood, bruises, or stains on clothing, as physical and sexual abuse often does. Even when a family appears from the outside to be functioning well a closer look within that family reveals that one sibling is emotionally abusing another.

Emotional abuse might be called "the sport of siblings," because so many brothers and sisters do it. Detecting it is complicated by the fact that both professionals and parents tend to accept emotionally abusive behavior as something that "normally" occurs in all children's interactions with their peers and siblings. The teasing and verbal put-downs that brothers and sisters engage in, although disliked by parents, is regarded by them as normal. "It's just kid behavior," they say, or, "All kids talk that way to each other." Usually it is excused as nothing more than sibling rivalry. The popular television show, *Roseanne*, bases much of its comedy on the verbally abusive behavior of the parents toward the children, as well as the children toward their siblings—as if this were perfectly ordinary. Maybe you have experienced this in your own life.

Although the three types of sibling abuse—physical, emotional, and sexual—are individually discussed and illustrated in these chapters, they often are all part of the same incident, the same family culture. Thus, you shouldn't think of each type as occurring only by itself. Emotional abuse often underlies physical and sexual abuse.

A survivor from Maine shares an example of abusive words accompanying hitting, slapping, or inappropriate sexual behavior:

> *I can't remember a time when my brother didn't taunt me, usually trying to get me to respond so he would be justified in hitting me. Usually he would be saying I was a crybaby or a sissy or stupid or ugly and that no one would like me, want to be around me, or whatever. Sometimes he would accuse me of doing something and if I denied it, he would call me a liar. I usually felt overwhelmingly helpless because nothing I said or did would stop him. If no one else was around, he would start beating on me, after which he would stop and go away. I felt helpless to stop any of it.*

In New Jersey, this survivor's brother, nine years older, used emotional abuse in connection with sexual abuse:

> *The emotional abuse stemmed directly from the sexual abuse. The earliest memory was when I was about five years old. I've blocked a lot of it out of my mind. But I always remember being afraid of being rejected by my parents. My brother was the oldest, and he made me believe that my parents would always believe him over me since I was only five and he was thirteen. So, you see, he always had some sort of power over me emotionally and physically. As a child and adolescent, I was introverted and never really shared my inner feelings with anyone. I felt like dirt and that my needs, concerns, and opinions never mattered, only those of other people. I was always in fear of both emotional and sexual abuse. I learned to prepare myself for both. I'm so resentful that I had to do this to survive mentally in my home. My brother would always present himself in these situations as being perfect—mature, responsible, brave—a model brother. Then I'd feel like an immature, not-credible child. He'd say things like how my parents thought he was so special, being the oldest. And that if I told on him, I would destroy the entire family; my parents would divorce. I would be sent to a foster home. He had such emotional control over me in that sense that I "obeyed" him and never told. He had control over my self-image and my body.*

Name-Calling

In my research on sibling abuse, name-calling was the most frequently reported form of emotional abuse. Perhaps you experienced this from a sibling.

Brothers or sisters often use name-calling to belittle or degrade their siblings. Name-calling generally focuses on an attribute or physical characteristic of the victim, such as height, weight, protruding teeth, red hair, freckles, speech, intelligence, the inability to perform a skill—the list goes on and on. For example, an Arkansas survivor told how her brothers called her "fatso" and "roly-poly" because of her weight. Another survivor reported that a dry skin problem prompted her siblings to call her "snake" and "crocodile."

A respondent from Montana describes the emotionally abusive name-calling she endured from a sibling:

I was heavy as a young child, about seven or eight years old. My brother called me "Cow." He was asked to mark all the children's socks with our names, so for mine he drew the face of a cow. He would also take a mistake I made and turn it into a nasty word game that he would call at me for years. A mistake was for a lifetime.

A Washington respondent writes:

My sister would verbally harass me—you're ugly, stupid, fat, etc. If I did accomplish something, she would turn things around and prove that I had failed or been a fool.

A man from Ohio who was called names tells of his experience:

I was left-handed and could not throw a ball very well. When we played softball in our neighborhood, my older brothers never wanted me to play on their teams. I was called names because of this. When they chose sides, they would never want me. Many times I would be left out of the game and would go home because they didn't want me. Of course, neither my brothers nor anyone else would help me learn to properly throw a ball. The same was true for coaches who taught gym classes. Their only concern was to win, win, win! To this day I hate sports! I thought a gym teacher's job was to help you learn to play sports. When I hear the word sports or coach today, I want to puke.

One respondent's father would call her names, and then the sibling would join in, with a devastating effect on the victim, as she recalls:

Name-calling usually was started by my father and picked up by my sibling. I often felt as though I was not a part of the family.

Ridicule

Ridicule is a form of emotional abuse that survivors remember with particular pain. Ridicule may be defined as words or actions used by a perpetrator to express contempt for the victim. Often ridicule is accompanied by laughter, as the victim, or something about the victim, is treated as a joke by the perpetrator.

One survivor of emotional abuse in the form of ridicule explained that her older sister had composed a song about her being overweight. The woman's sister sang the song, which rhymed, whenever she was in the victim's presence. The survivor talked about the humiliation she felt at school when her sister sang the song in front of her friends and the friends joined in, under the guise of simply "having fun." This ridicule was not fun for the victim, but a horribly painful experience that she still remembers vividly.

A 33-year-old woman wrote about the emotional abuse she received from a sibling, and its impact on her adult life:

My brother would tease me about not saying certain words correctly. Some words I could not pronounce correctly, so he would get me to say them and then would laugh at me. Now as an adult, I don't speak up when I should. I feel like people will laugh at what I have to say or they will think it's dumb.

Often a sibling's name inspired ridicule. One sibling abuse survivor wrote that she was called "Sewer," (as in a toilet outflow pipe) because her first name was Sue and her last name began with a "W." Something that she had not chosen—the name she had been given by her parents—had become the instrument of repeated ridicule by her own siblings.

Emotional abuse often does not occur alone but leads up to or accompanies physical or sexual abuse.

An adult woman tells of emotional abuse from siblings in a sexual context:

There was much teasing of a sexual nature from my brothers as I was going through puberty. Great fun was made of my wearing a bra and putting cotton in it. When I started menses, I would hide used Kotex in my radio so they would not tease me.

Other survivors describe the climate of emotional abuse in their childhood homes:

I was ridiculed by my older brothers and sisters for just being. Ridicule and put-downs were "normal" for our family.

My brothers loved to tease me to tears. They were ruthless in their teasing and did not let up. They teased me for being ugly. They teased me for being sloppy. They teased me for just being. This was the worst.

Let's pause for a moment and look more closely at these last two examples, because they provide information about how some people react to abuse from siblings.

There is a very dangerous hidden message in the "teasing" these two people went through. To be ridiculed for "just being" implies that it would be better if you "didn't be." To "don't be" implies a wish on someone's part that you were dead. The dangerous underlying message sent by the sibling doing the teasing is, "The world (or I as the perpetrator) would be better off if you didn't exist."

What a horrible message to hear! And how much worse when it comes from a member of your own family! Any victim of sibling abuse who does not act on this kind of malicious message (by committing suicide) has certainly earned the title of survivor. "Why was I ever born?" survivors might ask themselves—as if we had any power in the matter.

Parents often give their children the message to not exist without being aware of the implications of what they are saying. The transactional school of analysis, or TA, as it is called (made popular by Thomas Harris's book, *I'm OK—You're OK* and Eric Berne's *Games People Play*), refers to this as the game of "Don't Be."[7] In this "game," the parents imply in obvious or subtle ways that life would be better if the child were not around, for example, by remarking about how much less stress there would be, or how many fewer expenses.

When this emotionally abusive and manipulative "game" is analyzed from a reality perspective, it is easier to see its extreme emotional destructiveness. Children are not responsible for their existence. The *parents* brought the children into existence. Realistically, a child can do only one thing to comply with a sibling's or parent's wish that he or she did not exist. This vicious "game" sends the child a message of self-destruction, suicide, death. Remember this when, in a later chapter, we talk about how often the survivors of sibling abuse wrestle with depression, and how many have attempted suicide.

As one survivor reports regarding her parents' response to her sibling's taunts:

They just never thought about it or thought that it was harmful. They denied the evidence of my unhappiness and depression.

Degrading Comments

Another form of emotional abuse that aims at depriving children of their sense of dignity and worth is degradation. Many abuse survivors report that they were repeatedly told by their siblings that they were "worthless" and "no good." This emotionally devastating form of abuse carries with it a double-whammy, since degrading comments such as these affect the victim both at the time the abuse is occurring and continue to haunt the survivor well into adulthood.

Some people might say, "Oh, these things are forgotten when you grow up," but we often link the ways we act and feel as adults with the ways we acted and felt as children. For example, in order to excuse our adult deficiencies in art or music, we say, "I was never good at that when I was a child." It's the same with feelings. We say, "Ever since I was a child, I've cried easily," or, "He's always had a short fuse." As adults we carry with us the experiences of our childhoods, including occasions when we were the objects of degrading comments. Things that happen to us as children serve as the building blocks of our adult personalities.

To get a feeling for the devastating impact of degrading comments, as well as of emotional abuse in general, imagine that you are a small child again. Your world, and the security you feel in it, is centered on your relationships, at home with your parents and siblings, and at school and in the neighborhood with your peers. You are aware of what others think of you, and you want to be liked and valued, by your siblings and your peers. However, your brother or sister repeatedly tells you that you don't belong in the family and that no one really likes you, including your brothers and sisters, the other kids you hang out with, and anyone else who knows you. Obviously, this is a tremendous blow to your sense of self-worth, your self-esteem. If this assault on your dignity and personal worth continues, and your parents do nothing to put a stop to it, it can have an impact on you for years to come.

As one survivor describes it:

As a child, you believe everything you are told. It can last a lifetime.

A survivor from Washington was repeatedly degraded by an older sister when she was growing up:

I was being constantly told how ugly, dumb, unwanted I was. Already about two years of age I was told, "No one wants you around. I wish you were dead. You aren't my real sister. Your real parents didn't want you either, so they dumped you with us." I grew up feeling, if my own family doesn't like me, who will? I believed everything my sister ever told me—that I was ugly, dumb, homely, stupid, fat—even though I always was average in weight. I felt no one would ever love me.

A gay man suffered similar degrading comments from his brother:

My brother would tell me what a sissy or faggot I was; that I wasn't a man, and then would laugh. He would tell others to taunt me, to bait me. He would bring me to tears.

You may find that the emotional abuse you experienced as a child continues to characterize your adult relationships with your siblings. A child who was singled out for taunting with a negative nickname often continues to be taunted with it as an adult. Perhaps you are experiencing this now with a sibling, even though you're both adults. Do you still have to bear a derogatory nickname that was given to you as a child by your brother or sister? Does this nickname call attention to a physical characteristic or personality trait that made you different from your siblings? How do you feel about this nickname?

A woman from South Carolina, who has formed a support group for adults abused as children, still experiences emotional abuse from an older brother and sister:

They would tell me things like I was stupid and call me other names, make fun of me, make me do things I did not want to do, beat me up when I didn't do what they wanted. They made me feel I was not part of their family. They showed they loved each other but not me. And they still do this to me the same way, even at the age of 35.

A female physician in her forties who was emotionally abused by an older brother writes that the abuse has persisted into adulthood:

I can't recall a specific instance of emotional abuse. It was more of an attitude that still continues today. There is no sensitivity or openness from my brother. As a child I always felt I had to be "nice" and agree, or I would be yelled at or not accepted. As a child he wouldn't think of me as a person. Even now, there is no acknowledgment of me as an adult. But now I pity him more than anything because I see through his macho front and see a very insecure, immature, selfish, weak man who is threatened by my success and assertiveness. He still has a superior attitude. I do not see him. Our interactions are not meaningful or supportive—more formal or "proper." But he still calls me names if he doesn't get his way.

Another way one sibling degrades another is by "using" the victim. This form of abuse is similar to what was described in the last chapter, when older siblings controlled younger siblings with physical abuse and forced them to do what the perpetrators wanted. Likewise, emotional abuse—name-calling, ridicule, degrading comments—is often used to force a victim to comply with the perpetrator's demands.

The "use" of another sibling frequently occurs along gender lines, as when a brother sets himself up as "lord and master " over a sister. Most frequently, an older brother commands a younger sister to do things on his behalf, such as the household chores that he is expected to do. This type of behavior often occurs when older siblings are left in charge of younger siblings, such as after school, before the parents return home from work, or in the evening when the parents go out. The penalty for not complying with the perpetrator's demands may be physical or sexual abuse.

Respondents who suffered this form of emotional abuse said they felt that they existed only to do things for the older sibling, as if they were servants or slaves. This was especially true when the abuse occurred along gender lines, with an older brother forcing a younger sister to do his bidding.

A survivor who was raised on a farm in North Dakota in a very religious family of eight children reported that she had to wait on her older brothers in the house, even when she had been working all day in the fields. Her parents had instructed her to obey her older brothers in their absence. "It was as if my brothers could do no wrong," she reported. Her older brothers took advantage of her, not only by demanding that she do chores for them but by tricking her out of her allowance money. It only compounded the negative effects of this abuse when her parents paid no attention to the brothers' behavior. Eventually, the brothers' "use" of their sister included sexual abuse. The brothers took their parents' lack of attention as a license to treat her any way they wished.

Another survivor reports that the emotional abuse she received from older brothers has had a severe impact on her adult life:

I felt guilty bonding with other males and wasn't sure I could trust them. I felt crippling shame. I drank and acted out.

Another form of degradation experienced by people who participated in the sibling abuse study was being ignored—mentally erased—by siblings.

A victim from the West Coast got the erasure treatment from both older and younger brothers:

> *They totally ignored me. They did not want me along or around for anything ever. They would not talk to me or play with me.*

This survivor said that her brothers treated her this way because she was a girl—another example of abuse associated with gender. The problem of abuse based on gender (being male or female) recurs again and again throughout the accounts of survivors of not only sibling abuse but also abuse by parents and, especially, by spouses. Gender-related abuse is based on the incorrect and destructive assumption that males are somehow superior to females and thereby have a natural right to dominate them. This untrue and damaging myth will continue to contribute to society's willingness to allow girls and women to be abused by boys and men unless and until males are taught new lessons about being men. Men can be men without resorting to abuse, a lesson that needs to be taught at home and at school, in play, humor, relationships, commerce, government, public policy, and everywhere the destructive myth is subtly or openly supported and encouraged.

Emotional Abuse Intended to Motivate Behavioral Change

Strangely enough, emotional abuse is often initiated by a parent to motivate a child to change behavior the parent doesn't like, and is then picked up and mimicked by siblings. This kind of abuse occurs most frequently in two areas: 1) when a child is overweight; or, 2) when the child has sloppy personal habits. Names such as "fatso" or "pig," or degrading comments like, "You're a slob," are used by parents. These expressions are supposed to make the child want to change, but unfortunately, they work only to destroy the child's self-esteem. It is rare that serious behavioral change can be made by someone who feels worthless, ashamed, and degraded. Sometimes those feelings of shame just reinforce the disliked behavior because the person does it to get a kind of comfort that isn't available anywhere else. What is particularly sad is that siblings often take note of their parents' behavior and assume that it is all right for them to make these comments too, thereby adding to the victim's pain.

Intensifying A Fear

It is also a form of emotional abuse when one sibling intensifies, or exacerbates, or plays on another's fears in order to achieve control over the victim. Childhood fears that are commonly played upon include the fear of being lost or abandoned, fear of the dark, or fear of strangers. One might wonder at first how a perpetrator thinks of using a sibling's fear this way, but then one realizes that many parents use fear regularly to get children to obey or behave, for example, by telling children in a shopping center that if they linger behind, someone will take them away. Below are some examples of siblings committing emotional abuse by playing on other siblings' fears. Perhaps you can add to them from your own childhood experience.

One respondent in my survey reported being intensely afraid of a parakeet the family kept as a pet when she was growing up:

> *When we were in elementary school, my sisters would get the parakeet out of the cage and bring it near me. They would put it on my head so it would scratch me.*

This victim would panic whenever the bird came near her, and her sisters delighted in teasing her with it. The girl's only way to cope was to hide until her sisters tired of this activity.

One fear that older siblings have played on is a child's fear of getting lost and being unable to find the way home. An abuse survivor from Virginia recounted that her older brothers would take her into the woods and leave her there on her own. These repeated abandonments left her extremely frightened.

Another fear used by older siblings to threaten their victims was the fear of being eaten by wild animals or mysterious creatures—themes often found in fairy tales and children's stories. One survivor wrote that her earliest memories of fear-based emotional abuse dated from the first grade, when her oldest brother threatened to tie her to a tree and let the wolves eat her. He also threatened repeatedly to lock her out of the house so that the "bogeyman" would kill her. Obviously, whenever the older brother invoked these fears, he gained complete control over his sister. He could get her to do anything he wanted.

A survivor vividly described her fear of the dark, and the way her older sister manipulated this fear to force her to do household chores and otherwise dominate and control her. The sister would not allow the victim to share her bed at night unless the victim took care of the sister's household tasks. The victim was caught in a bind. Her parents were unaware of the arrangement, but she knew that if she told them about it, her sister would not let her into her bed. The victim would be left alone with her fear of the dark. Rather than let that happen, she acquiesced to her sister's domination and repeatedly suffered her sister's emotional abuse.

Destroying Personal Possessions

When you're a child, certain possessions are virtually part of you. They become part of your identity; you endow them with special value and meaning far beyond their true cost or condition. We can all remember a favorite childhood toy, book, or blanket. Some of us have kept these objects as nostalgic mementos. A perpetrator of emotional abuse learns to use these favorite things as instruments of abuse, based on the significance they have to the victim.

A 29-year-old woman remembers how proud she was of her tricycle. Her brother, three years older, used this favorite toy of hers to abuse her:

My earliest memory of being emotionally abused occurred when I was about four years of age. My brother took apart my tricycle and hid some of the pieces so it could not be put back together. I loved my tricycle and rode it practically every day. I was so hurt by the loss of this tricycle and by my brother's sense of satisfaction that he got away with it.

This victim's brother also damaged her dolls, ridiculed her, and called her hurtful names.

A Texas respondent experienced similar abuse from two older brothers:

They called me names. I was told my parents hated me. If my brothers found out I cared about something, for example, toys, they were taken and destroyed in front of me.

The personal possessions of this survivor from Massachusetts were destroyed by a sibling:

My sister used to take my things and wreck them, cut my clothes up to fit her and blackmail me to do her housework.

A survivor from Maine writes:

My brother would cut out the eyes, ears, mouth, and fingers of my dolls and hand them to me.

A man who was abused by an older brother reports:

A typical experience of abuse I suffered was my older brother would take whatever I had and destroy it. Then he would give it back, broken.

One man's vivid memory of being emotionally abused by a sibling is something you might hear a standup comedian tell, except for the deep underlying sadness it shows. This man's favorite childhood toy was a small cap with Mickey Mouse ears, bought during a family vacation at Disney World. The cap represented happy memories of an enjoyable vacation. In his account of it, he described how his brother took the cap from him and deliberately ripped off the Mickey Mouse ears, and then laughed about it.

Initially, one might find humor in a grown man's telling a woeful tale about a pair of Mickey Mouse ears that were torn from a cap he owned as a child. For one thing, the man could probably buy a dozen of these caps today. But the destruction of the cap is not the point. To fully understand and empathize with the survivor, several other factors must be considered.

First, the destruction of the hat was one of a series of abusive incidents the victim's brother directed at him, not a one-time event. (But remember, some single incidents *can* be harmful and identified as abusive, especially when they involve sexual abuse. One would ***not*** say that because a brother sexually molested his sister only one time, he had not abused her.)

Second, the destruction of the Mickey Mouse ears should be judged in light of the *deliberateness* of the perpetrator's action. Survivors of sibling abuse who participated in this research repeatedly called attention to the delight that their siblings took in destroying something that had been meaningful to them. The incident with the Mickey Mouse hat was no accident; the destruction was accomplished with a deliberation that made it abusive.

Finally, the incident should be considered in light of its impact on the victim, the target of the abuse. In this case, the victim was deeply hurt by his brother's behavior. Again, the destruction of the Mickey Mouse cap *per se* was not the point; rather, it was the effect of it upon the cap's owner. The statement people often make when something like this happens indicates how they experience its effect: "How could someone do something like this to *me*!" It is clear that the emotional abuse was directed not at the object, but at them personally.

Torture or Death of a Pet

The torture or death of a pet is similar to, but infinitely worse than, the destruction of a prized possession. But hurting or killing a pet involves the abuse of an animal's *life*. It takes a greater degree of cruelty to kill or hurt a living being, although the sibling victim's emotional pain may be the same. In some instances, the emotional pain may be even greater, because the message is clear that life—perhaps even the victim's life—has little meaning to the perpetrator. These survivors' remembrances of being emotionally abused through the destruction of pets may validate similar experiences for you.

A woman from Tennessee recalls her earliest and worst experience of emotional abuse at the hands of an older brother, more than twenty-five years ago, a memory that still causes her great pain:

> *My second oldest brother shot my little dog that I loved dearly. It loved me, only me. I cried by its grave for several days. Twenty years passed before I could care for another dog.*

The torture of a pet may occur in conjunction with other forms of emotional abuse as it did for this survivor:

> *My older brother would come to my room and tear up my toys. He would beat my dog after tying his legs together and wrapping a cloth around its mouth to tie it shut. My brother would tell me I was stupid and say, "Why me, why me? Why did I get a sister so stupid and dumb?" My brother also would tell me he hated me and wished I was dead.*

A 37-year-old male experienced this abusive incident from an older brother:

> *He took my pet frog and stabbed it to death in front of me while I begged him not to. Then he just laughed!*

Summary

Emotional abuse destroys its victims' self-esteem, and can make childhood a nightmare that follows them into adulthood.

A respondent recalls the nightmare of her childhood, which continues to affect her, so that as an adult she is plagued by low self-regard, is a compulsive overeater, has difficulty controlling her anger, and finds herself repeatedly involved in self-destructive relationships. She writes:

> *My sister would put me down at every opportunity. I couldn't compete because she was so much older than I. My parents often left me in her care. She manipulated my emotions and I would cry. I always felt inferior and wanted to run away. Throughout childhood I was tormented.*

Although the playground response to name-calling says, "Sticks and stones may break my bones, but words will never hurt me," the survivors' testimonies of emotional abuse presented in this chapter demonstrate that this saying is long on bravado and short on accuracy. Words *do* hurt.

A Task For You

Once again think back to your unpleasant or painful memories of being a child among your siblings. This time, don't focus on *behaviors,* meaning the physical acts a sibling directed at you, but rather on *words and the feelings you got from those words.* Did you go through any of the types of emotional abuse described in this chapter (also listed below)? If so, describe those experiences on a fresh page in your notebook.

Name-Calling

Ridicule

Degrading Comments (include awful nicknames your siblings gave you.)

Intensifying a Fear

Torture or Destruction of Personal Possessions or a Pet

Perhaps you experienced emotional abuse from a sibling in some other way. What was your experience of emotional abuse? Do you recall any especially painful memories of such abuse? Write about those memories in your notebook.

Endnote

[7] T. Harris, *Games People Play* (New York: Grove Press, 1967).

"My older brother sexually molested me numerous times when I was a small girl. He threatened to kill me if I told my parents. I was scared he would so I never told. I don't trust men to this day."

Chapter 5
I Can't Talk About It: Sexual Abuse

In an earlier chapter, you read a definition of sibling sexual abuse, and two types of sexual abuse were identified: contact and non-contact. Contact sexual abuse includes behaviors such as inappropriate touching, attempted penetration of any body opening with another body part or with an object, and vaginal or anal intercourse. Non-contact sexual abuse includes unwanted sexual teasing or taunting, indecent exposure, forcing a brother or sister to observe the sexual activities of another sibling (such as masturbation), taking pornographic pictures, or forcing a sibling to look at pornographic materials.

During a speaking engagement in San Francisco related to these definitions of sexual abuse, I made the comment that this form of abuse could range from inappropriate touching between siblings all the way to rape. A woman in the audience questioned my saying, "all the way to rape." She asked, "Hasn't a young girl's body already been raped when someone inappropriately touches her?"

This question made me realize that while rape is *legally* defined as forceful penetration, in reality *any* of the sexual behaviors referred to in our definitions are really a form of rape. This broader definition recognizes both the right of privacy for all persons regarding their sexuality and the seriousness of any verbal or physical violation of this right.

Even though usually the perpetrator is referred to as "he" and the victim as "she," remember that females are sometimes perpetrators and males are sometimes victims. Although research indicates that male sexual abuse perpetrators outnumber female perpetrators, more and more victims (both male and female) of female perpetrators are reporting their experiences of being abused. Unfortunately, our society still has difficulty acknowledging males as victims and females as offenders. The lack of support for male victims probably helps account for the fact that the majority of sexual abuse survivors in my sibling abuse study were female victims of male abusers.

Perhaps our definition of sexual abuse and the survivors' memories that follow will help you recall and rethink your own victimization. The accounts are organized under two headings: earliest memories of sexual abuse by a sibling, and typical experiences of sibling sexual abuse.

Earliest Memories of Sibling Sexual Abuse

Many of the participants in my research stated that the earliest incidents of sexual abuse in their childhoods occurred when they were five years old. However, this must be considered in light of the possibility that five is only the earliest age at which they can actually remember their victimization. In fact, although they might not be conscious of it, sexual abuse could have occurred even earlier. Some survivors, in fact, reported that they recalled having been sexually molested by siblings even as infants.

One respondent, for example, writes:

> *Sexual abuse was a part of my life from the time I was an infant. The age of three months is the earliest memory I have.*

In many instances, the initial episodes of sexual abuse escalated into more and different kinds of sexual behavior.

A survivor from Michigan writes:

> *I was three years old and I remember my oldest brother being in bed with me and rubbing against me in a way that I knew he shouldn't.*

A woman from California tells of her abuse, with severe consequences for her life:

> *About age three, my older brother started fondling me, which progressed to full sexual intercourse over the next years, starting when I was about nine or ten and continuing to age fifteen, when I ran away and became a hooker.*

A woman from Maryland recalls:

> *I was four years old and he (my older brother) told me he wanted to do something that Mom and Dad did. I refused. Then he offered to pay me a quarter and said that I would like it. If I turned him down, it was clear that he would hurt me. So I gave in and he made me perform oral sex with him.*

Another survivor writes that her earliest memory involved touching through clothes:

> *It's difficult to pinpoint the first time or close to it that the sexual abuse occurred. After being in therapy, I still cannot remember. The earliest possibly was when I was four. It could have been earlier. It was mainly my brother*

making me touch his erection through his underwear and he touching my vagina in my underpants.

A respondent from Texas tries to recall the first episode of sexual victimization by her siblings:

I know there was abuse before this, but I can only remember pieces of it. This is the first time I can remember. I was five years old. My brothers and I and two other boys were there. My brothers sold me to the two boys and they sexually abused me. When the oldest brother forced me to touch him and put his penis in my mouth, I got sick. This made him mad. He hit me and put his pocket knife at my throat and sexually abused me. Then the other brothers repeated the same acts as the oldest brother. Both urinated on me and locked me under the house, where I was tied to a pole with no clothes on. They let me out before my parents arrived home. This is all I can remember.

The absence of any sexual information from parents, including instruction on "empowerment," or the right to say "No" to unwanted touches, often set up the victim for abuse from an older sibling.

A young woman from Missouri describes her first sexual abuse by a brother who was eight years older:

I believe the first time was when I was six years old. He was babysitting me because the rest of my family was out somewhere. He came to my aunt's to pick me up, and he walked me home. I knew something felt different. He was holding my hand in a protective sort of way. It felt nice to have my brother taking care of me. We got home, and he showed me his penis and wanted me to touch it. After that I don't remember much, except he started masturbating and he ejaculated into the trash can. I was scared because I didn't know what was happening to him.

That survivor's memory identifies one of the most common opportunities for sexual abuse to take place: when an older sibling was babysitting a younger sibling after school or in the evening.

This survivor went through a similar experience.

He was babysitting me and my younger sister. She was in the tub. We were watching TV. He offered me money. He performed oral sex on me.

Although sibling sexual abuse most often occurs with a male as the perpetrator and a female the victim, sometimes a male perpetrator chooses his

This man remembers being abused over a long period of time by his brother:

> *I don't remember when it began, but it started with me giving him oral sex. I usually masturbated him. I remember this happening on Sunday mornings because Mom and Dad would be gone to Grandma's house.*

Frequently, the sexual abuse was accompanied from the beginning by threats of physical violence from the older sibling, either to make the victim comply or to enure the victim's silence.

Threats enabled the perpetrator to control this victim for subsequent abuse:

> *I was about twelve years old. My brother told me if I didn't take off my clothes, he would take his baseball bat and hit me in the head and I would die. I knew he would do it because he had already put me in the hospital. Then he raped me.*

Another survivor writes of being threatened with a beating:

> *He would lay me down and put his big fist by my face, and he would say, "If you scream, this is what you'll get." Then he would sexually abuse me.*

A survivor from Texas writes:

> *I was seven, and my eldest brother took me into the woods while my mother was working. He then wanted to "play dirty" with me. He touched me on my nipples, then touched me on my vagina. He then made me touch his penis. After it was all over he said, "If you tell anyone, I will kill you." I believed him and was frightened.*

Another survivor describes being threatened by her brother, who was 14 years older:

> *My brother threatened to kill me if I told our parents about him molesting me. I was three or four years of age at the time; he was about 18. He showed me the butcher block with the bloodied ax that we kept in the basement for butchering chickens. He said he would kill me there if I told.*

Perpetrators often blame their victims for the sexual abuse. By blaming the victim, a perpetrator seeks to protect himself and excuse his failure to take responsibility for his own inappropriate behavior. Frequently, this attitude seems to be endorsed by society at large, as expressed in the most common responses to the plight of rape victims. People ask, "How was she dressed?" "What was she doing in that neighborhood?" "Why did she go to his apartment?" ***How a woman was dressed, or where she went, did not give anyone permission to rape her.*** The same principle applies to sibling abuse.

Too often, sibling sexual abuse victims are blamed for what happened to them, not only by their perpetrator but also by their parents. When the victim is a child, it is difficult to hold on to the reality of her own experience in the face of denial and blame by other important people in her life (parents and siblings). Often the victim accepts the blame, resulting in deep feelings of guilt and shame, which the victim may carry with her throughout her life.

This woman's mother knew about the abuse and blamed her, not her brother:

> *I was about eight years old. My mother and stepfather had gone out for a few hours and my brother told me he wanted to imitate something he had seen between adults. He took my skirt off and was kissing and fondling me. He then laid on top of me and was rubbing himself against me, mimicking intercourse. This went on for about an hour until my mother came home and caught us. As was the usual case in my home, she didn't say anything to my brother and pinned all the blame on me for what happened.*

A survivor from Indiana describes her earliest memory of being sexually abused:

> *When I was about nine, my brothers and I and some of their friends were watching TV. My brother was under a blanket on the floor, and he invited me and a friend to join him. When I did, he fondled my genitals. Then he went over to his friends on the couch and bragged about what he had done.*

The perpetrator of sibling sexual abuse frequently uses trickery to involve the victim, as this woman's brother did:

> *About age ten my brother approached me to engage in "research" with him. He told me he was studying breast feeding and needed to see mine. He proceeded to undress me and fondle my breasts.*

Another woman who was tricked by an older sibling into a sexual encounter writes:

> *I was about six to eight years old. My oldest brother called me to come up the street to his best friend's house. They told me they had a new game to play. They told me to pull my pants down and to lie down under a table that was covered with a sheet so no one could see. Then they took turns rubbing their penises all over my lower body. I don't remember if there was penetration. They threatened me not to tell anyone. I don't remember much about it. I did not tell anyone. I remember a vague feeling that my brother was more important than me and I should keep quiet and do what he wants.*

This survivor, now the mother of a 3-year-old girl, states that she has taught her daughter the difference between good touches and secret touches. It is this kind of instruction that, unfortunately, many sibling sexual abuse survivors never received, even though it might have prevented the abuse they suffered.

A Kansas survivor writes that it was very "painful to dig out of my repressed childhood" her memory of sexual abuse. She describes her older brother, the perpetrator, as her parents' "golden haired" son, their favorite child:

> *I was ten or eleven, in fifth or sixth grade. My parents were out of the house. My brother came into the bedroom saying, "Do you want to feel something good?" Remember, this guy was "God" around the house, and here he was paying attention to me. So we went to bed. I remember it hurt. I was a virgin and he said it wouldn't hurt for long. He climaxed, and I was left hurting physically and mentally.*

Another survivor, from Arizona, shares the memory of being sexually abused on vacation: recalls that the first time she was sexually abused was during a vacation trip, when she and her brother, a year older, shared a bedroom.

> *My earliest memory is of my brother sneaking into my bed while we were on vacation and we were sharing one bedroom. This happened while my parents were still out on the town. I pretended I was asleep, and it was very difficult to determine what to do about it because of the physical pleasure but inappropriate and selfish behavior on his part.*

The sexual encounters continued after they returned home, with her brother coming into her bedroom at night when their parents were asleep.

Sexual abuse can arouse pleasant physical feelings in the victim. This is a natural body response—it's what your genitals were made for. When a person responds to sexual stimulation, it shows that his or her body is working correctly. Sexual response can be like laughing when being tickled. The victim may be aware of these pleasurable feelings despite the greater feelings of guilt and shame. Later, if the abuse is discovered by a parent, the perpetrator may play on these normal body reactions to sexual activity. The perpetrator may say to the victim, for example, "You enjoyed it. Why didn't you stop it?" Unfortunately, parents often accept this rationalization, and the victim is blamed for what happened, and revictimized. The victim is forced to deal with her shame and guilt by herself.

A 42-year-old woman describes her first sexually abusive encounter with her brother:

I remember waking up as my brother was touching me. I was so scared!

This woman speaks for many sexual abuse survivors.

Typical Experiences of Sexual Abuse

Very few of the victims of sibling sexual abuse who participated in the study indicated that the sexual abuse was a one-time event. In most cases the episodes were repeated, and the perpetrators went on to other kinds of sexual abuse, often accompanied by physical and emotional abuse. Sexual abuse by siblings is repeated over and over, resembling the experience of children who are sexually assaulted by adults, such as fathers or other adults known to the child. The assaults generally continue in a compulsive or repetitive manner until the victim is old enough to prevent them, the perpetrator leaves the household (to go to college or join the armed forces, for example), or the sexually abusive behavior is discovered and appropriate interventions occur.

One survivor writes:

I can't remember exactly how the sexual abuse started, but when I was smaller, there was a lot of experimenting. He would do things to me like putting his finger in my vagina. Then as I got older, would perform oral sex on me.

Another respondent writes of a quick progression to more intrusive forms of abuse:

Initially I was forced to masturbate him one night, but from then on it moved quickly to oral sex on him and eventually he raped me.

A 48-year-old Idaho woman reports on how she was groomed for abuse with games:

It began as games and grew to "look and feel." As I became older, he played with my breasts and then fondled my genitals, always wanting but never achieving intercourse. He showed me with his fingers how it would feel.

A Kansas survivor describes the various forms of sexual abuse she experienced from an older brother:

He started the activity by fondling me and progressed to having me manually stimulate his penis. After the initial two incidents, I refused to cooperate further. He then began to expose himself to me when we were alone and try to force me to participate. My refusal led to a stage of terrorism, where he would chase me and threaten me.

In addition to using trickery and threats, a common tactic for brothers was to isolate their sisters so that they could sexually abuse them.

One sister reports that her older brother always knew when to attack her:

He would always seem to know when I was alone and when no one could hear. I would always know when he entered a room if it would happen. He would make me terrified. I would think, "Oh, no, not again!" He would try to compliment me in a sexual way. Complimenting a 4- to 6-year-old on her "great breasts" was not what I'd call a turn-on. He would either undress me or make me undress myself. He would undress and make me touch his erection. I hated that because he would force me to do it and would hold my hand against it to almost masturbate him. He never climaxed, though. He would touch me, almost like he was examining me. A few times he had oral sex on me ... and I was always so scared because my muscles were so tight and my opening was so small. He never really could enter without severe pain. I would say he was hurting me, which he was, and I'd cry in hopes he would stop. Sometimes he did. Other times he would force himself inside of me and I would hurt for days.

Similarly, a woman from Michigan writes about her brother's use of isolation:

One thing my brother always did was to isolate me. He was always saying, "Come over here. I want to show you something" or "Come on, let's go for a ride."

Another technique brothers used to isolate their sisters was to involve them in games like Hide and Seek. The older brother would invite the younger sister to hide with him "in a really great place, where they'll never find us." He would then use the opportunity to sexually abuse his sister.

While sibling abuse often takes place when an older sibling is babysitting a younger sibling, after school or in the evening when the parents were away, sexual abuse can also occur at night.

This survivor tried to avoid being abused at night, but to no avail:

I would try to put off going to bed. I would try to cover up tight with my blankets. It didn't help. My brother would come into my room and touch me all over. I would pretend I was asleep. After he left, I would cry and cry.

When sexual abuse from a sibling occurred at night, a victim's common defense was to pretend to be asleep. Knowing that she was both physically and emotionally powerless against her attacker, and that resistance was futile, a victim would act as if she were sleeping. This behavior may also have been a psychological defense against emotional pain and suffering, as if she were saying, "If I'm asleep, I won't be aware of what is happening. It won't hurt me as much."

Two survivors write:

> *My brother would come into my room at night and fondle my breasts and genitals. He used to put his fingers inside me and would put his penis between my legs. He never tried to penetrate me with his penis. I always pretended to be asleep.*

> *Typically, my brother would sneak into my bed in the middle of the night and experiment on me. I would stir and try to scare him away by pretending to wake up, but he was undaunted. He would wait until I seemingly fell back to sleep and start again—vaginal penetration or oral sex.*

One survivor's sexual abuse began when she was three or four years old. Her brother, thirteen years older, forced her to perform oral sex on him:

> *I had already learned that if I cried out in pain he would beat me worse, so I had to remain silent until he left. The abuse continued through the years—sometimes in his car, sometimes in my room at night. I was terrified of him. I was terrified to go to my room at night. I wedged myself on the cold linoleum floor (cold Connecticut winters) between my bed and the wall, trying to hide from him at night and stay awake so the nightmares wouldn't come. It was the family joke that I must keep falling out of my bed at night.*

Up to this point, all but one of the sexual abuse survivors who have described their abuse have been women. Men can also be the victims of their brothers or sisters, however. Unfortunately though, men are taught to present a tough front and to be able to handle their own problems, which may prevent them from acknowledging their victimization and seeking help.

This man has bravely stepped forward to tell about his experiences of being sexually abused by his brother:

> *My brother caught me masturbating once. That's when the sexual abuse began. At night he would have me fondle him, masturbate him, and fellate him, depending on what he wanted. He threatened to tell Mom about catching me masturbating if I didn't go along. The abuse went on about a year or two. It was always at night. He would lie on his back. A street light would*

shine across his body through the curtains, and he would call me to come "do" him. I felt as if I were on stage with the street light and trapped in a bad part. I hated him immensely. Finally, after a year or so I told him he could tell whomever he wanted, but I wouldn't do it anymore. The abuse stopped, but the damage was done. My feelings would haunt me into high school, college, and my marriage.

The incidents of sexual abuse described so far have consisted of masturbation, oral sex, or intercourse. But other survivors reported inappropriate touching or sexually slanted comments, acts which also represent the rape of an individual's sexual privacy and personal dignity.

These three individuals shared their experiences of this kind of sexual abuse:

My brother, two years older, would commonly grab my chest where my breasts were developing and would twist. When I would ask him to stop, he would say, "You love it and you know it."

When I was in my teens, my brother would say provocative things to me to see how I'd respond.

My brother would come up behind me and grab my breasts. He would verbally harass me and constantly make sexual references, even when we were older teenagers.

The feelings of survivors as they recall their sexual victimization by a sibling can best be summarized by two final comments:

It's too much to even put into words on paper.

I still feel so hurt and sad for that poor little defenseless girl. They raped her—she suffers still.

Summary

Two types of sibling sexual abuse have been discussed in this chapter—contact and non-contact. Sexual abuse between siblings is most often accompanied by threats, in contrast to sexual abuse by an adult. Older siblings threaten younger siblings that if their parents are told, the older sibling will do serious bodily harm to the younger. By comparison, sexual abuse between an adult and a child usually occurs in the context of the adult's telling the child that he or she is special, and that what is happening should remain a secret between them. The effects of sexual abuse, however, are the same regardless of context or the age of the perpetrator, as we shall see in a later chapter. Sexually abused children continue to experience the effects of their victimization in adulthood.

A Task for You

Think now about unpleasant sexual encounters you might have had with a brother or sister when you were growing up at home. These may have been of a contact nature—touching, oral sex, intercourse—or of a non-contact nature, involving indecent exposure, unwanted sexual comments, or pornographic materials. As you think back on these experiences and briefly describe them on a fresh page in your notebook, don't try to explain or account for your own participation in these activities, whether or not you experienced them as pleasurable (which you may well have), or why you were involved. We will talk about that later. At this time, simply recall and describe any activities of a sexual nature in which a sibling took part. Remember to include both non-contact sexual experiences with a sibling (indecent exposure, unwanted sexual comments, being forced to watch a sibling masturbate or view pornographic material, etc.), and sexual experiences with a sibling that included physical contact (touching, oral sex, intercourse, etc.).

"My parents would just ignore the constant physical and emotional abuse from my older sister. I felt so alone when they would not intervene."

Chapter 6
When Parents Are No Help

While you were reading the survivors' accounts in the previous three chapters, you might have seen yourself in some of their descriptions of physical, emotional, or sexual abuse. Perhaps you also identified with some of the remarks made about parents, for example, when a parent started name-calling and then siblings joined in, or when parents were absent when abusive behavior was repeatedly inflicted by the sibling who was left in charge, or when parents ignored or failed to believe reports of abuse or, even worse, blamed the victims.

While you read the next two chapters, think about your parents. Focus on whether or not they knew about the abuse you were suffering, and, if they knew, what they did about it.

This task might make you uncomfortable. A small voice in the back of your mind may remind you to "Honor thy father and mother," or at least to avoid anything that might seem like disrespect toward your elders. But by reading this chapter, looking for comparisons to your own parents in the descriptions, and completing the task at the end of the chapter, you are *not* dishonoring your parents. You are working to uncover events that actually occurred, and attempting to understand what happened. You are confronting reality, instead of trying to ignore it and enduring the serious consequences of pretending that it didn't happen (discussed in a later chapter).

This perspective might make you uncomfortable for another reason as well. Looking at how your parents might have been involved in the sibling abuse you experienced could conflict with ideas you have about how wonderful your parents were, how special you were to them, or how well they treated you. Many survivors have difficulty letting go of their family illusions, even when proof of an abusive environment exists.

To attempt to *understand* what caused your parents' responses to your abuse by a sibling is not the same as *blaming* your parents. You might be very angry at them for having failed to recognize that abuse was going on, or for ignoring it when you told them. However, after you have read this chapter and completed the task at the end of it, perhaps you will better understand what occurred, your parents' awareness of the problem, and the reasons for their response or their failure to respond.

In the next chapter, we examine in more detail what might have been going on in your parents' lives that kept them from providing the protection you needed. Remember, you cannot change what has happened, but *you can take responsibility for your own life from now on*, for your journey of healing. Our goal in this chapter is not to assign blame but to realistically examine what happened, and to attempt to frame the abuse you suffered in a way that you can understand and use for your own personal growth.

After first looking at how aware parents were of the abuse, this chapter discusses parents' responses according to the most typical ways they were reported by the 150 participants in my research on sibling abuse, as follows:

- ignoring or minimizing the abuse
- blaming the victim
- joining in the abuse
- disbelieving that abuse was occurring
- responding inappropriately to the abuse

Parental Awareness

When you were growing up at home and experienced the physical, emotional, or sexual abuse that you identified in the last three chapters, did your parents know what was happening? Compare your answer to this question with those provided by the sibling abuse study participants.

Nearly two-thirds of the survivors of physical and emotional abuse felt that their parents knew that abuse was going on, understandably so, since it is difficult to hide physical or emotional abuse from other family members. The parents must have witnessed at least some of the hitting, slapping, name-calling, ridicule, or other forms of physical and emotional abuse.

On the other hand, fewer than one-quarter of the sibling *sexual* abuse survivors could say with certainty that their parents were aware of the abuse. This finding is also understandable, however, for a whole host of reasons:

- Sexual abuse does not occur in the presence of parents, but when parents are away from home or during the night when parents are sleeping.

- Sibling sexual abuse is generally accompanied by threats to gain compliance and ensure secrecy. An older brother threatens bodily harm to his sister if she reports the molestation to their parents.
- The emotional climate in some families prevents the victim from telling the parents anything, let alone that a sibling is sexually abusing him or her.
- Frequently, a small child does not understand that the sexual activity an older sibling forces on him or her is abuse.
- Victims often blame themselves for sexual abuse by a sibling.

Ignoring or Minimizing the Abuse

A typical parental response to sibling physical and emotional abuse is to ignore or minimize it. Often, they excuse the behavior on the basis that it is merely sibling rivalry. "Boys will be boys; children will be children," victims are told by their parents. While, yes, all brothers and sisters do fight and call each other names, *abuse* of one sibling by another in a way that is deliberately harmful and repeated or that is sexual in any way is not normal. Nothing excuses or justifies sibling abuse! Ignoring or minimizing sibling abuse gives the perpetrator permission to continue victimizing his or her sibling and leaves the victim without hope or help.

A survivor from California illustrates this parental minimizing reaction, in discussing the physical abuse she experienced from a brother:

> *They ignored or minimized the abuse. They told me, "Boys are boys and they need to clear their system."*

Obviously, this response did not help this young woman while she was being repeatedly victimized by her brother. She must have felt incredibly helpless and abandoned by her parents who inappropriately excused the abusive behavior as part of normal development, and, in essence, gave the brother permission to continue.

Another survivor reported that her parents responded to her complaints about her brother's physically abusive behavior by minimizing what he was doing, saying, "He doesn't know his own strength." This response amounted to telling the victim that she would just have to accept the abuse and again, it gave the perpetrator permission to continue his behavior.

A 33-year-old survivor reports that, when she told her parents about the physical abuse she was suffering at the hands of an older brother:

My mother would say that he (my brother) was not hitting me hard enough for me to complain, or, she would say that he is going through a stage and would outgrow it.

The permission granted to this perpetrator by his parents' response certainly influenced his later behavior. For instance, this survivor went on to report that when she was eight, her brother pushed her down a flight of stairs, and after that would repeatedly throw her to the floor and hit her in the stomach or on the arms.

A man from Wyoming who was physically abused by an older brother describes his parents' response:

I told them once, and they didn't believe me, and they would leave me alone with him again. Then I really suffered for telling on him. I soon learned not to tell.

A Canadian woman experienced this reaction from her parents to the physical abuse she was experiencing:

My parents had no reaction to anything except denial. My mother may have made a token effort to stop it but she was very ineffectual.

A survivor of emotional abuse from a brother writes:

My parents saw it as normal sibling rivalry and did not correct any of what my brother said. If they were around when it was occurring, they would just say we had to learn to get along better.

This survivor suggests some courses of action her parents might have taken:

They could have talked to my brother to help him realize how hurtful his teasing and name calling were. If this did not work, they could have forbidden this kind of behavior and punished appropriately. Perhaps they could have been a better role model themselves.

A Tennessee survivor says of her parents:

It wasn't abuse to them. It was normal. Our abuse of each other as siblings disturbed their own peace, and so they'd yell or get in on it, too. Then, when Mom and Dad were not watching, the big boys would get even anyway and it would be worse, so I just as soon didn't want Mom and Dad "protecting" me or Mom and Dad getting into another fight with each other—a vicious, escalating, abusive, cycle of insanity!

This testimony gives us a glimpse into the emotional climate in some homes where sibling abuse took place. Abuse was the usual way family members related to each other, with little interest in the needs and concerns of others. Instead, everyone had to look out for him- or herself. Family members got what they needed or wanted by dominating others. The parents were abusive to each other, they were abusive to the children, so why shouldn't the siblings in turn be abusive to one another? Violence can be a learned behavior. In many cases, the habit of using it has to be acquired from someone else—and unfortunately, in many families children adopt violent ways of interacting from the example set by their parents.

These three survivors share examples of the climate in their childhood homes:

My father was so emotionally abusive to us, especially to my brother, that he probably wouldn't have noticed that there was anything wrong with the way my brother treated me. My brother in essence was doing to me what was done to him.

My brother constantly belittled me, telling me how stupid, incompetent, ugly, useless, etc., I was. But again, he was only modeling our mother's behavior.

My parents were abusive too, so it was just part of everyday life.

Some survivors' parents not only excused abusive sibling behavior but felt that it was good for the victim. "It will make you tough," one father told his daughter when she complained that her two older brothers relentlessly teased her about being ugly.

A Pennsylvania respondent wrote that her parents knew that her older brother was emotionally abusive toward her, but that they "framed their reaction in such a way that it seemed OK." Her parents would tell her, "The smartest one keeps quiet. All kids fight." Another survivor wrote that whenever she reported being emotionally abused by her sister, her parents would tell her, "Sisters must love each other!" The survivor added in large letters, "GREAT!" as if to say, "What good did that do for me?" It's obvious from her comments that the sister's emotional abuse continued.

An Ohio survivor recalled that her parents accepted the emotional abuse she was suffering from a younger sister by laughing it off.

An Arizona survivor describes her parents' similar reaction:

> *Everything was always a joke to them. They laughed at my emotions. Usually their reply was to tell me to quit complaining and that I would get over it.*

An Indiana woman recalled that her mother condoned emotional abuse by a sibling because she herself had been raised in a home where physical abuse had been tolerated. The victim's mother excused the behavior by saying that what she saw her children doing was not as severe as what she had experienced in her own childhood. Again, the message was that abusive behavior was normal and acceptable.

Still another survivor, writing about her parents' indifference to the emotional abuse she suffered from her brother, describes the effect it had on her:

> *Both of my parents minimized my brother's angry, aggressive behavior, especially my mother, who I don't think knew what to do. I received little support from my parents. I often went to my mother for her to intervene, but she made minimal efforts. I soon began to feel very powerless as a child and felt that I had to just put up with my brother's abuse.*

Blaming the Victim

Some parents accepted the reports of sibling abuse, but blamed the victim for what was happening. When parents blame the victim, the victim is revictimized by the very people who were supposed to help! Perhaps you experienced being blamed or revictimized yourself. (Another way victims are revictimized is by blaming themselves for their victimization, something which will be discussed in a later chapter.) When children report abuse to their parents but are blamed for it themselves, the perpetrators are not held responsible for their actions, but instead are presented with the message that their behavior is okay because the victim somehow deserved to be abused. Again, the perpetrators in essence are given license to continue.

The respondent who was tickled until she vomited reported that when she told her parents about this abuse by her older sister, and about repeated episodes of punching and shoving, her parents remarked, "You must have done something to deserve it." Rather than examine what had happened between the siblings, the parents made the victim feel guilty, as if she had been responsible for what had occurred.

Many of the arguments and fights between siblings that escalate into physical and emotional abuse may have started out with both parties contributing. There is some truth to the saying, "It takes two to tango." One theory of sibling abuse, the interactional theory, supposes that the way some children interact with others makes them especially prone to being abused. This theory does not blame victims, because that would absolve perpetrators of responsibility for their actions and place the burden of guilt on the victims. Rather, the interactional theory suggests that some victims should be shown that certain aspects of their own behavior may prompt or provoke abusive responses from their siblings.

Here's an example: six-year-old Heather went into her 12-year-old brother's room and took one of his comic books to look at without Corey's knowledge or permission. While she was looking at it, the cover got crinkled. When Corey found out, he slapped her face, punched her in the stomach, and then locked her in a closet for three hours. Clearly, Heather had done something wrong in taking Corey's book without permission. Just as clearly, Corey's response was inappropriate and abusive. A child must be taught not to take other people's property without asking, but physical abuse is not the way to teach that lesson. Children who whine and pester their siblings may also evoke an abusive response. Again, an abusive response is an inappropriate way to deal with children who are trying to learn how to get their needs met, and the abusive sibling should be held accountable for his or her behavior. At the same time, the behavior of the whiner is a contributing factor in the interaction. Both people must be responsible for their behavior. No one deserves or asks to be abused.

This victim was blamed for her sibling's abusive behavior toward her:

> *I was hurt by the abuse I received from a younger sister, but my sister was not blamed or it was turned around that I had done something to cause it. She was never wrong.*

Another survivor said that her parents would attempt to intervene whenever she and her siblings fought. Her parents usually managed to stop the conflict, but then, since she was the oldest, she would be accused of having caused the disturbance and told that she should set a better example. Unfortunately, the survivor reported, she had no idea how to end the physical and emotional abuse she received from her younger siblings.

A 40-year-old survivor quotes her mother's response to physically abusive behavior by her two brothers, five and eight years older:

Mom would say, "You should know better than to be there. You should know better. They don't."

A typical inappropriate parental response is related by a Texas survivor abused by an older brother and sister:

It started when I was ten or eleven. My sister would hit me and then my mother would hit me because she said I deserved it if my sister hit me. I always tried to be good, but a lot of times it seemed like for no reason this would happen. It was as if my mother was giving my sister permission to treat me as she saw fit.

A woman who survived physical and emotional abuse by her older brother reports:

Most of the time the abuse was happening, I lived with my divorced mother. I'm not sure she knew what was happening. But even if she did, I don't think she would have stopped it. Her philosophy was that you must take what men and life dished out to you and you didn't complain because you probably did something to deserve it. My mother treated all her daughters with disrespect and had none for herself, so my brother learned early in life that he didn't have to respect us either. The abuse finally stopped because I ran away from home when I was sixteen and never came back.

This sexual abuse victim was blamed for being molested by an abusive brother:

When I hinted that I was having problems with my brother, they placed the blame on me or they ignored it. My mother once walked in on us and beat me up. She told me I was a slut, that I deserved it.

A man who was sexually victimized by an older brother writes that although his parents were not aware of the abuse, he never doubted what their response to it would have been:

Since I was the "good son" in the family—an excellent student, always helpful, never in trouble—I would have received all the blame and been the target of their anger. They would have said that I should have known better and that I could have stopped my brother. He would have been yelled at, but would not have received the same treatment that I did.

Joining in the Abuse

Perhaps the saddest parental response, especially to emotional abuse such as name-calling and ridicule, occurs when parents join the sibling perpetrator in abusing the victim. By doing so, the parents may not intend to be malicious, but instead hope to force the victim to change whatever undesirable traits or behavior inspired the abuse in the first place. For example, children may be called, "slob," or told that they keep their rooms like pig pens, in an attempt to motivate them to be neater in their personal habits. Ridicule provides no motivation for behavioral changes, and its effect on a victim's self-esteem is usually devastating.

When a child seeks its parents' protection from physical or emotional abuse by a sibling, but instead the parents join in the abuse, the child is victimized anew, with no one left to turn to for protection. Victims suffer feelings of intense sadness, loneliness, and vulnerability, as they stand unprotected from further abuse.

A survivor from Ohio describes what happened when her oldest sister emotionally abused her:

My mother would pick up on it and also make fun of me.

An Arizona survivor recalls that her family just piled it on when they heard about a group of peers taunting her:

When I was six and started school, the girls took me in the bathroom and put me in the toilet to wash me. Then they called me, "Stinkweed." I was crushed. When I got home, I talked about it. Even my whole family laughed at me and called me that daily. It still hurts. It's something I'll never forget. They still remind me of it.

Disbelief That Abuse Was Occurring

The survivors in my research study wrote that their parents frequently responded to complaints of sibling sexual abuse by refusing to believe them. The result? Further victimization. The abused children become victims of their own parents' disbelief. They are revictimized by their parents' failure to protect them from the perpetrators' continuing behavior.

A survivor from New York was revictimized this way after reporting sexual abuse by her brother:

When I tried to tell my father about it, he called my mother and brother into the room, told them my accusations, and asked my brother if it was true.

Naturally, my brother said I was lying and my mother stood there supporting him. I got a beating later by my mother for daring to say anything and for "lying." My brother knew that from then on, there was nothing he couldn't do to me. He was immune from punishment. Never again did I say a word, since to do so would only have meant more abuse from them both. I concluded it was better to keep my mouth shut.

A male survivor recalls his parents' disbelief at his accounts of physical abuse, and the difficult position this placed him in when the abuse became sexual:

When I tried to tell them about the beatings I was taking, they didn't believe me and they would leave me alone with him again. So when it came to the sexual abuse, I didn't think they would believe me.

Responding Inappropriately

Among the families chronicled in my survey, some parents discovered that one of their children was abusing another. Or they at least believed it when the abused child told them it was happening. But there was no happy ending for these abused children because their parents responses were either ineffective or made the problem even worse.

One common inappropriate response was that the parents would become abusive toward the perpetrator.

A physical abuse survivor explains what happened in her family when an older sister was caught being abusive to her:

My parents would yell at her and pinch and bite her to "teach" her how it felt so she would stop doing it. It only made it worse for me though.

This "disciplinary" approach is based on the myth that giving the perpetrators "a dose of their own medicine" inspires them to change their behavior. In fact, this sort of discipline is more likely to have just the opposite effect. According to the theory that violence begets violence, this form of parental discipline only encourages continued abuse. The perpetrator will only become angrier as a result of this discipline and can be expected to ventilate this anger on the parent or a sibling.

Another reported inappropriate parental response to sibling abuse was the use of severe corporal punishment on the perpetrator. One respondent reported that when she told her parents about being physically abused by her older brothers, her father beat her brothers.

She describes her own reaction to her brothers' beatings:

My older brothers received a severe beating when I told my parents how they were abusing me. The severity of the beating, however, discouraged me from ever reporting again what happened because I wanted to avoid a more violent outcome.

This victim's attempts to report physical abuse to parents set up further violence throughout the whole family:

My father would never know about the abuse I experienced because my mother would never tell him for fear of what he would do. She would try to hide it from him. She would say, "Don't tell your father; don't get him started."

Similarly, a California survivor writes:

On a couple of instances my father did know about my abuse from an older brother when I cried out in pain. Once my father beat my brother in front of me. Once he yelled at my brother for hours about not hitting a woman. When my brother started crying, my stepmother went to comfort him. My father then hit her in the face for taking my brother's side.

A Montana survivor describes her father's response to abuse among her siblings:

Dad would yell at us and threaten us with a belt if we didn't shut up. His anger was directed not at my brother who abused me but at all the kids. I learned to cry silently because of my dad. The belt was worse than my brother's abuse.

A different, but just as inappropriate, parental response was described by a Washington survivor. When she reported her older siblings' emotionally abusive ridicule and degrading comments, her parents replied that her siblings were just jealous of her, and told her that God would eventually reward her for being good. This ineffective response just allowed her siblings to continue abusing her.

A Tennessee respondent, referring to her home life as a "death camp existence," describes what would have happened if her parents had discovered that her brother was sexually abusing her:

There would have been more beatings for everyone all around. Instead of at-random sort of violence, there would have been a concerted and pointed effort to make us children even more miserable.

Summary

In this chapter, we have reviewed various parental responses to abusive behavior between siblings. You have been encouraged to think back to your own parents' response to your abuse by a sibling and compare what you experienced with the sibling abuse survivors who participated in this research. The parental responses to sibling abusive behavior that were discussed included ignoring or minimizing the abuse; blaming the victim; joining in the abuse; disbelieving that abuse was occurring; and responding inappropriately to the abuse.

A Task for You

Now it's time for you to think again about the physical, emotional, or sexual abuse you experienced from a sibling and your parents' knowledge of and response to this abuse.

First, turn to a fresh page in your notebook and please answer the following questions (answer yes, no, or I don't know), depending upon the type of abuse you experienced from a sibling (you may have been abused in more than one way):

1) If you experienced physical abuse from a sibling, were your parents aware of what was happening?
2) If you experienced emotional abuse from a sibling, were your parents aware of what was happening?
3) If you experienced sexual abuse from a sibling, were your parents aware of what was happening?
4) Listed here are the five parental responses most often cited in this chapter by sibling abuse survivors.

A. My parents ignored or minimized the abuse I was suffering.

B. My parents blamed the victim—me.

C. My parents joined my sibling(s) in abusing me.

D. My parents refused to believe that I was being abused.

E. My parents responded inappropriately to the abuse.

In your notebook write down each response and a sentence or a few phrases about how it applied to your situation. Skip any responses that don't apply to you or your parents. Think about the questions below to help you consider your parents' responses.

- *How was this response played out in my family?*
- *What incident(s) do I recall that illustrate this response?*
- *What do I remember my parent(s) saying that provides an example of this response?*

"My mother had so many problems of her own when I was growing up that I can understand why she didn't know what my brother was doing to me; however, that doesn't take away from the pain of his abuse and the effects it's had on my life."

Chapter 7
Beyond Blame: Understanding My Parents' Response

In the last chapter, you had the opportunity to begin to examine your parents' responses to the physical, emotional, or sexual abuse you remember receiving from a sibling as you were growing up. We focused on whether or not your parents were aware of the abuse and, if they were, how they reacted. In this chapter, we consider why they responded as they did.

Remember, our aim is not to *blame* your parents for their responses. Rather, our goal is to *understand* what was happening, because with understanding you can more fully uncover the extent of the abuse you experienced and begin the path toward healing the effects of this abuse on your life.

As in previous chapters, you will be able to read accounts from sibling abuse survivors that give examples of what was happening in their own parents' lives while they were being abused by siblings. Perhaps by identifying similarities in your experience with some of these survivors' stories you may gain insight into your parents' lives at the time your sibling was abusing you.

Viewing Parents from a Reality Perspective

We had no role in selecting our parents. This simple, even naive statement carries a depth of meaning. We didn't choose our parents, and consequently, we just accept them as a "given" in our lives. When we hear the word "parents," the people we know as "mother" and "father" come to mind. They are the only parents we have ever had, and, unless we acquired a step-parent during childhood, the only persons we think of when we hear that term.

We don't usually think of our parents as unique individuals with stresses, problems, crises, pleasures, and joys of their own. We tend to view their lives as constant or static. We see only our own ups and downs as we were growing up. It is rare for children to appreciate that our parents experienced ups and downs of their own or to see clearly how their problems had an impact on our childhood lives.

At the end of this chapter, you will be given a task that will encourage you to view your parents in a different way than you have been accustomed to. At this point, however, let's look at some of the factors that sibling abuse survivors have identified which relate to the abuse they suffered from their siblings. These comments may help you understand what might have been going on in your parents' lives at the time you were being abused by your sibling or siblings.

Inappropriate Expectations

As you have already learned from survivors' accounts in earlier chapters, physical, emotional, and sexual abuse often occurs when an older sibling has been left in charge of a younger sibling. For instance, the older sibling might be babysitting for a younger brother or sister while their parents are away from home, either after school before the parents get home from work, or at night when the parents are out.

It's not at all unusual for an older sibling to take care of a younger one. Babysitters can be expensive, and many communities don't have latchkey programs for children who get home from school before their parents arrive from work. However, when parents leave a younger sibling in the care of an older one, safeguards must be in place. Rules must be established to govern what the children are allowed to do in their parents' absence, covering such matters as which appliances may be used, what foods and beverages may be consumed, whether friends may enter the house, etc.

Also, parents need to regularly monitor and evaluate this arrangement of leaving an older sibling in charge of a younger one. Evaluations should be held with each child individually because, as you recall from an earlier chapter, sibling sexual abuse usually occurs in a context of threats, and with the older sibling present, a younger child will be too afraid of being hurt to tell their parents that he or she has been abused by that older brother or sister.

A 43-year-old woman from Massachusetts writes:

When my parents went out dancing or to my aunt's home on a Saturday night, my two older brothers babysat us six children. Not long after they left, my brothers would tell us to go to bed. It was too early, so we didn't want to go to bed. When we resisted, we were hit. I was punched and slapped by my oldest brother. If I defended myself by hitting back, my oldest brother would grab my wrists in the air as he screamed at me that he would hit me more.

He would be telling me what to do and to go to bed. I would be crying hard even more and would go to bed.This survivor told her parents what was happening, and they instructed her brothers to allow the younger siblings to stay up. But the abuse persisted and eventually escalated to include sexual abuse. When the survivor was ten years old, she told her parents that she had been sexually molested by one of her brothers. After that, the parents hired a babysitter whenever they went out for the evening.

Another survivor reports:

My mother would go to play bingo leaving my sister who was three years older in charge with specific chores to be done. My sister would make us do the work. If it didn't get done when she said, she would hit us with a belt. Leaving her in charge gave her every right to do whatever she wanted.

A survivor recalls her experiences of being watched by an older brother when her parents left the house for an evening out:

He would constantly be telling me to do something for him like ordering me around, to change TV channels, to get him something to drink, make popcorn, prepare a sandwich, etc. My refusal or sometimes just being too slow to comply would merit me being hit, usually open-handed, but sometimes with a closed fist.

An Ohio survivor describes what happened whenever she was left in the care of her older brother after their mother died:

My father would go to work or out on a date and my brother would be watching TV. I would be in my room, and he would come to my room with a stick and some cord. He would beat me with the stick and then tie my hands behind my back and tie my feet together. If I screamed too loud, he would put a scarf in my mouth or tie it around my mouth. Once he took a big pot of boiling water and poured it on my hand. He did so much to me, I've blocked some of it out of my mind.

Parents Overwhelmed by Their Own Problems

Often, parents were overwhelmed by their own problems and were not aware that their children were abusing their siblings. The parents' own problems were more than they could handle, so they didn't want to take on the additional problems the siblings were having with each other. Additionally, they may have lacked the energy or skills to handle the situation, so instead they minimized or simply ignored the abuse that was occurring. Many sibling abuse survivors reported that their parents were coping with alcoholism, mental illness, or marital difficulties, problems that interfered with their ability to effectively intervene in the sibling abuse.

A Nevada survivor describes the chaotic conditions in her home when she was growing up:

> *My mother was never home for eight or nine years of my most important years. She probably wasn't aware of too much in our home, as she was drinking. She'd stay away for weeks at a time and leave us there with my brother ten years older.*

A California survivor describes a similar situation in her childhood home:

> *My family was very chaotic. My father was an alcoholic. My mother died when I was eleven years old. My father had many lovers and was gone a lot of the time.*

A Washington survivor writes that her mother could not control her sister's abusive behavior toward her, and that her father had problems of his own:

> *My father was always too drunk to take note of the abuse or gone to the local tavern getting drunker.*

Chronic mental or physical illness may so consume a parent's energy that children are left unattended or in the care of an older sibling unable to handle the responsibility.

A survivor from Pennsylvania describes this kind of situation:

> *I don't think my mother knew how badly I was being hurt by my older sister and I was afraid to tell her for fear of retaliation. Mother was busy trying to survive on practically nothing and deal with her own emotional problems. Also, she probably had systemic lupus then, even though it wasn't diagnosed until years later. I think she didn't want to know how bad things were because she was powerless to change her circumstances.*

Some survivors wrote that their fathers were not involved in what was happening at home because they had to work more than one job to support a large family. In some instances, the fathers were physically present but psychologically absent

Fighting Violence with Violence

Every form of sibling abuse is violence. You might have thought that only physical abuse fit that definition, because hitting, slapping, pushing, etc. are such obviously violent acts. But emotional and sexual abuse are just as violent. They are injurious and harmful, and violate a person's dignity and self-respect.

In the previous chapter, many survivors reported that their parents reacted to sibling abuse by responding ineffectively or, worse, violently. Rereading their accounts may help you understand better how the members of these families related to each other. The families described earlier operated within a whole context or culture of violence. Fathers were abusive to mothers, or vice versa; parents were abusive toward their children; and the children in turn abused each other. You may have experienced this when you were growing up.

In families like these, violence becomes a method of problem-solving—not a very good method, since it creates more (longer-term) problems with short-term solutions. When a problem arises among family members, it isn't dealt with in a deliberate or thoughtful manner. Rather, violence occurs. There is hitting, slapping, or other violent behavior, or violence is expressed in words, with family members shouting, calling names, and making degrading comments about each other. When the children become involved in conflict with their siblings, they follow the only example they have—their parents—and use violence (abuse) to resolve their differences. Theorists who define violence as a *learned* behavior would say that these children have *learned* this method of problem-solving from their parents. Psychologists also refer to this as *modeling*. Parents serve as role models to their children when they engage in abuse, and by observing their parents, the children learn to copy the abusive behaviors.

These survivors' accounts illustrate the family culture of violence that is learned by the children:

> *My parents were so busy abusing themselves and each other and us that it was a part of our everyday life.*

> *My mother abused me physically and emotionally also. She thought I deserved beatings from her and from my sister.*

A 36-year-old Indiana survivor describes life in her childhood home:

> *My parents abused me as bad if not worse than my brothers did. I would miss weeks of school at a time because of bruises, black eyes, etc. I didn't think they would be able to stop my brothers from hurting me when they did it themselves.*

As this survivor writes, children who have been abused by their parents or a sibling often repeat this behavior in their own relationships, unless they learn new and non-violent ways to relate to others:

> *As children we were physically abused by our parents, as I look back on the way we were disciplined and treated in general by them. I experienced a lot of abuse from my older brother—going back as far as I can remember. Then I would turn around and abuse my sister. I would get her twice as hard as what I received. The older we got, the worse it got.*

Thus, violence or abuse became an accepted or normal form of interaction in some families.

A 46-year-old survivor, currently in counseling for emotional problems that she now realizes stem from childhood abuse by two older brothers, comes to this conclusion:

> *I truly thought as a child that abuse was normal until last year when I started seeking counseling.*

Similarly, a survivor from Washington writes:

> *The abuse was considered normal behavior by my parents, who had no idea what normal might be. I might add that the physical abuse by my siblings was much less than the emotional abuse by my parents.*

A New York participant in the sibling abuse study pointed out that sibling abuse does not occur in a vacuum—it is a learned behavior. Further, violence can be learned not only within the family, but from movies and TV, where it is often portrayed as an appropriate and satisfying way to deal with conflict. Mental health professionals today are concerned that we witness so much violence in the media that we become desensitized to it, and that, in time, we begin to accept violent behavior as normal behavior.

As this sibling abuse research participant writes:

> *My mother was as abusive toward me as my brother was. He simply followed her behavior. My mother, in a sense, taught him how to abuse me and gave him permission to do so, as she did.*

In their unhelpful and nonprotective responses to the abuse occurring between their children, some parents may have been acting in accord with their belief that it's good for a child to get the anger out of his or her system, to express it rather than bottle it up within. While it is helpful for us to be aware of our anger, the raw expression of rage does not in itself promote resolution of the problems that cause that anger. Even if you feel temporarily relieved, nothing at all has been actually solved by this behavior.

As human beings, we are endowed with a brain and the ability to speak. We can communicate with others regarding the emotional impact of their behavior on us and thereby learn to resolve and avoid such conflicts. This dialogue is called problem-solving. Unfortunately, it is a skill too rarely understood or used in families. Instead, when conflict occurs, family members verbally or physically lash out at one another. Eventually, the emotions may return to normal, but because nothing has been learned from the outburst, the conflict will return.

Summary

In this chapter, we have focused on trying to understand what was going on in our parents' lives that might explain why they failed to deal appropriately with our abuse by a sibling. Having to deal with personal problems, however, does not excuse their ignoring or rationalizing the abuse (physical, emotional, or sexual) we experienced. Although we may understand and even appreciate the difficulties our parents faced, this does not ease the pain we suffered then, or the emotional pain that we, as adults, continue to feel as the effect or aftermath of this abuse by a sibling.

A Task For You

Now it is time for you to look at your own family. In the task at the end of the previous chapter, you were asked to determine whether your parents were aware of the abuse you were experiencing from a sibling, and, if they were aware, *how* they responded. In this task, I want you to think about *why* they responded as they did. Again, the goal is not to *blame* your parents but to *understand* what was happening in your family and through this understanding to facilitate your own healing process from the effects of abuse.

Think of the period of time when the abuse you might have experienced was most severe. If the abuse took place throughout your childhood, but you cannot recall one specific period of time (for example, when you were in junior high school) that was more significant than another, then focus on a specific incident or series of incidents for this exercise.

The statements below will direct you down a path of memory. You may want to read one of these statements, then close your eyes and visualize your life at the time referred to. Be factual. The purpose of this exercise is not to talk you into believing that you were the victim of sibling abuse, but to encourage you to examine events that actually occurred.

- First, select a particular period of time in your childhood when you were being abused by a sibling. Try to remember how you looked, the way your hair was cut or styled, a specific outfit you wore, a familiar toy or bicycle. You might find it helpful to look at some photos taken at this time in your life. *(Spend a few minutes on this process.)*
- Next, visualize yourself going to school—waiting for the school bus, walking with friends to school, or being driven to school by your parents.
- In your notebook, name a few of your friends.
- Visualize your classroom, some teachers, the lunchroom or cafeteria, the gym, the locker where you kept your books. *(Spend a few minutes doing this.)*
- Now visualize yourself back home again. What did your house look like on the outside? *(Spend a few minutes thinking about each of the next directions.)*
- In your mind, go into the house and look around inside.
- Enter your room and familiarize yourself again with that setting. Do you remember the color of the curtains, your bedspread, pictures on the wall, or favorite mementos?

- Now go back to the living room and visualize your parents or the person(s) responsible for your care.
- Continue your memory journey by writing in your notebook a brief *physical* description of your mother.
- Now write a short paragraph describing your mother's *personality.* How did she come across to you and to others?
- During the time you identified earlier, when you were being abused by your sibling, what significant events were going on in your mother's life? What emotional crises was she dealing with? For example, was she experiencing depression, an unhappy marriage, stress at being a parent or from a job, pressure from having to care for elderly parents, problems with in-laws or other family members? Briefly identify and describe in your notebook these significant events in your mother's life.
- Now write a brief paragraph giving a *physical* description of your father.
- Write a paragraph in your notebook describing your father's *personality.* How did he come across to you and to others?
- During the time you identified earlier, when you were being abused by your sibling, what significant events were taking place in your father's life? What kind of crises was he dealing with? For example, was he experiencing job-related stress, depression, a problem with alcohol or drugs, an unhappy marriage, problems with in-laws or other relatives? Briefly identify and describe these significant events in your notebook.
- Review what you wrote after Chapter 6 about whether your parents were aware of the abuse and how they responded to it. Based on what you wrote and the questions you have just answered, write a short statement about *why* you think your parents responded as they did to the abuse you were experiencing.

"As an adult I have used food and alcohol to cope with the terrible feelings I have about myself. I was told as a child by my siblings I was dumb, stupid, and ugly. I have lived out these words. Therapy is helping me turn my life around."

Chapter 8
Recognizing the Effects of Sibling Abuse In My Life

L**et's briefly review where we** are at this point. We have read the accounts of many sibling abuse survivors describing how they were physically, emotionally, or sexually abused by a sibling. Also, we have examined the ways these survivors' parents responded to their abuse. I hope that reading these accounts has helped you determine whether or not the treatment you received from a sibling as you were growing up should be considered abuse. I hope, too, that you can begin to understand (although not excuse) your parents' responses to your experiences at the hands of your siblings.

Now it is important to understand the impact or effect that childhood experiences of sibling abuse may have had on your life. Again, we will rely on the testimony of some of the 150 survivors of sibling abuse who participated in my research project. Reading their statements will help you determine the impact abuse has had on your life. Reading this chapter will help you make some important decisions regarding your journey of healing.

This chapter is organized according to the ten most common ways in which abuse from a sibling has affected survivors' adult lives:

- poor self-esteem
- problems in relationships with the opposite sex
- difficulty with interpersonal relationships
- repeating the victim role in other relationships
- continued self-blame
- anger toward the abuser
- problems in sexual functioning
- addictions
- depression
- post-traumatic stress disorder

Sibling abuse survivors who participated in my research were asked to identify the ways they felt their abuse had affected them as adults. In the following pages, the survivors tell how their lives as adults—some twenty, thirty, forty or more years later—have reflected the violence inflicted on them as children by their siblings.

As you read these pages, think about yourself and the abuse you suffered. At the end of the chapter, you will be asked to identify how the abuse has affected your life.

Poor Self-Esteem

Nearly every sibling abuse survivor who participated in my research, whether victimized by physical, emotional, or sexual abuse, referred to his or her poor self-esteem and related it to having been a victim of sibling abuse. Low self-esteem appears to be a universal effect of not only sibling abuse but also abuse that children receive from parents and other adults. As do other survivors of childhood abuse, the respondents to the sibling abuse survey feel unwanted, inferior, unloved, and inadequate and they connected these feelings to their sibling abuse experiences.

Survivors write:

If someone says something hurtful or gets angry, I think they will stop loving me.

I lack self-esteem and self-confidence. I cling to my husband and am afraid of a lot of things.

I am unsure of my abilities. I lack assertiveness for fear I might verbally be assaulted.

A middle-aged survivor, who as a child was emotionally abused by two older brothers, states:

The abuse contributed to my low self-esteem and self-confidence. I still have difficulty accepting credit for successes. I have a continuing sense of being worthless and unlovable, despite evidence to the contrary.

Survivors of emotional abuse, especially in the form of name-calling and degrading comments, often appear to have personalized the messages contained in the abuse. This phenomenon is known as a "self-fulfilling prophecy," in that the victim behaves in such a way that he or she acts out the qualities implied by the degrading names or comments. Many of the names and degrading comments addressed to the survivors focused on physical characteristics such as their weight or general appearance.

A survivor who was repeatedly told by her older brother that she was ugly and fat writes:

I have a hard time believing I am a slender, attractive woman. At times I feel that I'm fat and ugly, but I know I'm not.

The survivor you read about in an earlier chapter who was called "cow" by her brother because of her weight problem is still affected by this emotional abuse as a 39-year-old woman:

I think part of my weight and eating-disorder problems are from believing I was a cow and cows are fat. I have a low self-image and self-worth, and at one time they were so low, I didn't believe anyone would care if I was alive or not. I'm still on antidepressants.

Sexual abuse survivors often report that their feelings of worthlessness are associated with guilt and shame, a combination that frequently ends in self-blame for their victimization.

This survivor attempted to cope with these feelings with religion:

I felt dirty. I sought baptism and religious experiences to cleanse me.

Problems in Relationships with the Opposite Sex

Women who were physically, emotionally, or sexually abused by their brothers report that the abuse in their childhoods affects their ability to form relationships with men. These survivors find themselves distrustful, suspicious, fearful, and even full of hate when relating to men. What appears to happen is that survivors transfer their feelings toward their abusive brothers to men in general.

The transference process doesn't apply only to experiences of sibling abuse. For example, if the first dog you encounter as a child greets you by taking a bite out of your leg, you are going to transfer this experience to other dogs by being distrustful of them. Unfortunately, this distrust prevents you from ever opening yourself up to a positive or corrective experience. In the case of female sibling abuse survivors, their victimization affects their ability to relate to men and, especially, to form intimate relationships with men. In some instances, survivors reported that this influenced their decisions never to marry.

One survivor writes:

> *I am uncertain of men's real intentions. I see them as a source of pain.*

Similar feelings can be found in the words of an Idaho survivor:

> *Other than my husband, I am not comfortable in the presence of any man in any given situation without knowing I have a way out.*

A California respondent shares her discomfort around men:

> *I have a lot of fear of men and tend to use my mind and intellect to push men away and intimidate them the same way I was intimidated. I have a lot of difficulties in my relationships with men. I tend to disagree a lot and to be very afraid/contemptuous of a man's need for me.*

A Chicago survivor writes:

> *I do not trust men. I fear them. I have been unable to marry. I choose inadequate men to be involved with. I have a fear of intimacy.*

Even sibling abuse survivors who have married report that they are having problems in their marital relationships, and that these problems stem from a pervasive sense of distrust of members of the opposite sex, including their husbands.

One survivor describes how difficult she finds it not to view her husband as being like her emotionally abusive brothers:

> *I overreact to my husband's actions. Sometimes I doubt his motives for doing things, and I accuse him of being like my brothers. I learned not to trust men. I believed they were all evil.*

Some female survivors have described their feeling toward men as a fear of entrapment. It's possible that this fear stems from having been physically restrained by their abusive siblings—tied up, pinned to the floor, etc.—while the abuse took place. The fear may also stem from having felt trapped within their family, especially when their parents failed to protect them from their abuser's torments. As we have seen, the survivors themselves were often blamed, heightening their feelings of entrapment.

Some survivors' discomfort with men has affected their spiritual or religious life. Perhaps you have experienced this or something like it. In the Judeo-Christian tradition, God has always been depicted as a male figure. Male pronouns are used in scriptures and prayers that refer to God. Many survivors find it difficult to conceptualize a male God as being loving, kind, and good, when their childhood relationships with males, in the persons of abusive brothers or, in some instances, fathers, were altogether devoid of goodness, kindness, and love.

One survivor, who was physically abused by her only sibling, an older brother, bears the psychic scars in the form of an extreme fear of men, which has influenced even her religious practices:

Prior to more than three years of counseling, my concept of God was very warped. I saw Him as someone who was out to destroy or terrorize me.

Sibling abuse has its effect on male victims, too, in their later ability to establish and sustain relationships.

A 36-year-old male reports that his marriage is affected by the abuse he experienced from a sibling as a child:

It ruined whatever self-esteem and self-worth I could muster. It drove me away from people in school, thinking no one would like or love me if they knew the real me. This attitude is still prevalent today. This, combined with the parental emotional abuse, has just about totally ruined my life. It has affected my marriage immeasurably because I feel like if I get close, I'll get hurt. So right now, thirteen years into marriage, I honestly haven't got an intimate relationship.

Similarly, a middle-aged male who was physically abused by his brother describes how the abuse has affected his marriage:

I was a victim. As an adult I created another victim. All the anger and resentment I had in me I took out on my wife. She took all she could take. She is now divorcing me. I've lost the best thing that ever happened to me.

Difficulty With Interpersonal Relationships

Some survivors reported difficulties in forming relationships not only with members of the opposite sex but with anyone, regardless of gender. One woman stated that the abuse she experienced in her past affects her present-day relationship with her own child, and that "often I have been too hard on my son."

She and several other survivors emphatically stated that they would never have more than one child, so that there would be no opportunity for sibling abuse in their families.

It is hard for me not to repeat patterns of learned behavior. The verbal abuse is the hardest one for me to stop. I'm very aware of defending my boundaries. I'm still struggling to give my son his own boundaries; however, my son and I have continued therapy to help us be individuals. I'm too fearful of enmeshment and repeating earlier cycles to rely on my subjectivity, to intercept what I'm too close to see. I doubt my parenting ability.

This survivor's remarks incorporate two important points about violence: violence can be a learned behavior, and violence is likely to be repeated in a family through generation after generation *unless* the family learns more effective interpersonal relationship skills. This pattern of abuse being handed down, with children inflicting abuse on their own children, is known as the "intergenerational cycle of violence."

The difficulty respondents have in interpersonal relationships is often related to their low self-esteem, as it is for this survivor:

> *I do not stand up for myself. I accept things without questioning.*

A Washington survivor describes the impact of the abuse on her interpersonal relationships:

> *I find it difficult to relate to others. I am not afraid of people or hate them. I merely find no desire to reach out to others socially or emotionally. Mostly I simply want to be left alone.*

A middle-aged divorced woman from Maine who was abused by both a younger and an older sister describes the effects of her abuse:

> *I'm angry. I feel my self-esteem has been diminished. I act out in more sophisticated, socially acceptable ways. My anger is directed toward peers at work as though they were my sister.*

Other survivors describe their reactions:

> *It has made me very cynical, untrusting of those who attempt to get close quickly. I grew up feeling if your own family doesn't like or want you, who will?*

> *I get very afraid and shrivel when anyone is physically forceful with me. Even if they are being playful or rough-housing, I get terribly upset and tremble.*

> *It took me until my third year of college to really realize and get under control my own rage when frustrated, to really act upon not yelling at my roommates, threatening them, or throwing adult temper tantrums.*

The inability to handle anger appropriately is a significant problem that sibling abuse survivors bring to interpersonal relationships. Note how often in the preceding accounts the survivors use the words *anger* and *rage*. Their difficulties with anger include an inability to express any anger at all, fear of other people's anger, and fear of their own seemingly uncontrollable outbursts of rage. The survivors related their present anger to three stages of their lives: 1) the anger they felt as *children* about their abuse, which they were often unable to express because of their parents' inappropriate responses; 2) a continuous feeling of generalized anger throughout their *adult* years, the source of which they often did not know until they sought professional help; and, 3) the anger at their sibling that they still experience *today* for the abuse they suffered as a child.

The difficulty some survivors have in their interpersonal relationships is shown either in overt conflict with other adults or in overcompensating for feelings of low self-worth by trying too hard to please others; either method of coping interferes with their ability to form good relationships.

A midwest survivor of emotional abuse by both older and younger brothers writes:

> *Until I went into psychotherapy one year ago, I did everything I could to be approved of by my family—worked all the time, spent money for their needs, etc., just to have them tell me I was OK. They continued to downgrade my profession and my education. I was always trying to be perfect and took all responsibility for my family. Unfortunately, I married someone who had two adult children who treated me as my brothers did, and I went through the same dance for them too.*

Repeating the Victim Role

A significant aftereffect of sibling abuse is that, as adults, survivors often enter into relationships in which they are revictimized. As if on purpose, the survivors choose friends and mates who place them in situations where they can again become abuse victims. This phenomenon is the product of their low self-esteem and feelings of worthlessness. It is as if they went through life wearing "kick me" signs, like the victim who describes herself as a "doormat" in relating to others.

A California survivor, abused by her brother and sister, writes:

> *It took me into my thirties before I began to see a pattern from the abuse I experienced from an older sister. I chose a first husband who abused me. Also, I tend to constantly be doing too much, as if to make me feel better.*

Similarly, another survivor writes:

> *The abuse from my childhood made me think that was normal. It made me stay in an abusive adult relationship and think it wasn't so bad. It took a long, long time until I was able to call for the police to come to our home, and then only after much counseling.*

An Indiana survivor also traces her tolerance for adult domestic violence to being abused in childhood:

Being abused by someone I thought I was supposed to love set me up for further abuse from mates. I developed very unhealthy boundaries. I suffered through three years of abuse in my first marriage.

Continued Self-Blame

The victims of sibling sexual abuse often blame themselves for the abuse (frequently because they have been told over and over by the perpetrators and/or their parents that it is their fault), and as survivors, they keep on blaming themselves into adulthood. Perhaps when you think back on your own abuse, you find that you feel a measure of responsibility for what your sibling inflicted on you. Repeatedly, survivors believe that they allowed themselves to be sexually abused, though in reality there probably was nothing that they could have done at the time to prevent it. Perpetrators play on this self-blaming tendency. When accused or confronted, a perpetrator will often say to the victim, "You could have stopped it if you'd wanted to," Or, "You seemed to enjoy it too."

An Idaho survivor was made to feel responsible for her sexual abuse by an older brother, and notes the effects it has had on her adult life:

I was told by several women and especially by my older sister that it was my fault, because of the way I dressed and carried myself. I am very self-conscious now as an adult of how I dress. I do not like or wear short skirts. I prefer turtleneck sweaters and high-necked blouses. I do not accept compliments very well from men.

At the age of four, one respondent was paid a quarter by her older brother to perform oral sex. She complied, largely out of fear that, if she didn't, he would harm her.

She writes:

I have punished myself for twenty-two years for taking that quarter from him. I don't like myself.

This painful acknowledgment, along with a statement from a survivor in Arizona who says she feels guilty for not having been able to prevent her traumatic childhood, shows how our past childhood beliefs, even when they're not logical, can negatively affect our lives well into adulthood. These illogical beliefs (such as "It's my fault because I took the quarter") are called "thinking errors," or "toxic thinking," or less formally, "stinking thinking." The survivor confuses what actually occurred with what *should* have happened. The survivor then assumes the full blame for what happened because what *should* have happened did not take place (the abuse was not prevented). In fact, the circumstances were probably such that there was little that the victim could have done differently. Even if she had refused the quarter, she might have been abused anyway. The perpetrators always have more power than the victims. This survivor had not been empowered by her parents to say "No" to sexual assault, and her parents did not protect her. Therapy can help survivors evaluate such beliefs on a rational basis and modify them when it is appropriate.

Anger Toward the Perpetrator

Sibling abuse survivors report that the abuse they experienced as children has particular effects on their adult lives in the anger they repeatedly experience. For some survivors, this anger is generalized, expressed with sporadic outbursts in response to any number of greater or lesser provocations. For others, the anger is more specifically directed at men or women who remind them of their abusers.

How angry do the survivors feel toward their abusive brothers or sisters? In thinking about how you feel toward the brother or sister who physically, emotionally, or sexually abused you, you might be able to identify with these survivors. Each participant in the sibling abuse study was asked to rate his or her anger toward the abusive sibling on a scale ranging from one to five, with one indicating that they were "not at all angry" and five that they were "very angry." More than half of the survivors of all three types of sibling abuse indicated that they were "very angry" at their abuser, and several wrote in higher numbers than five, to denote the intensity of their anger toward their sibling abusers.

Descriptions the survivors gave of their angry feelings toward their abusers indicate how few of them have been able to lead normal, emotionally healthy lives. Many respondents described the hours they've spent in therapy, a process that for some has been very painful, as they have struggled to come to grips with the effects of abuse on their lives.

Although many survivors indicated how angry they still were toward their abusers, others stated that they were no longer angry at all. You might feel this way too. There are several possible explanations for this response. Some survivors have already completed psychotherapy, and have worked through their anger toward their siblings. This doesn't necessarily mean that they have forgotten what happened to them, but they have made peace within themselves for the abuse they experienced.Some survivors may not feel angry because they are denying to themselves the existence of that anger. Let's look at a comparable situation. Research shows that children who are the victims of their parents' alcoholism learn early in life that it is not safe to experience and share feelings of fear, embarrassment, loneliness, and anger. Other family members will not accept or validate these feelings. Therefore, the children learn to engage in an ongoing and thorough process of denial, in order to survive the problems and stress created by their parents' alcoholism. They pretend to be happy, and deny—or are out of touch with—the reality of their emotional pain. For some survivors of abuse, the denial process continues into adulthood, and creates problems in their everyday lives. Therapists report that denial of emotional pain by the children of alcoholic parents frequently prevents them as adults from seeking professional help for their resultant emotional problems. For some—and you may be able to identify with this—their denial takes the form of blocking out most childhood memories. It is as if they simply cannot remember what happened to them when they were children.

Likewise, research involving the survivors of sexual abuse by adult family members indicates that, while the survivors often experience overwhelming feelings of shame, guilt, despair, and anger toward their abusers, they handle these feelings most commonly by denying them. It's as if the feelings are just too painful to recognize.

Sibling abuse survivors, especially those who were sexually abused and couldn't tell their parents because they'd been threatened by the perpetrators—or whose parents did not believe them when they did report the abuse—may be in a similar situation. They too were forced to deny their anger at what was happening to them. Like some adult children of alcoholics and survivors of adult sexual abuse, many sibling abuse survivors have difficulty remembering specific details about the abuse. The memory of these events is so painful that they cannot or do not wish to revisit it.

A 38-year-old Massachusetts woman writes about her difficulty in remembering:

> *I'm realizing how sketchy my memories are of my abuse. I guess like most people, I've blocked out an awful lot of it.*

Dr. Harriet Golhor Lerner, in her book *The Dance of Anger*, describes the ways many women who have been victims of various types of abuse attempt to handle their anger:

Most of us have received little help in learning to use our anger to clarify and strengthen ourselves and our relationships. Instead, our lessons have encouraged us to fear anger excessively, to deny it entirely, to displace it on inappropriate targets, or to turn it against ourselves. We learn to deny that there is any cause for anger, to close our eyes to its true sources, or to vent anger ineffectively, in a manner that only maintains rather than challenges the status quo. Let us begin to unlearn these things so that we can use our "anger energy" in the service of our own dignity and growth.[8]

Lerner maintains that anger is always the result whenever a person is victimized, taken advantage of, manipulated, or used. Unfortunately, people generally manage their anger in ways that are ineffective in the long run, including silent submission, ineffective fighting and blaming, and emotional distancing.

Although her book is not addressed specifically to them, Lerner provides valuable advice for sibling abuse survivors in suggesting that people ask themselves two questions:

1) What unresolved and unaddressed issues with an important other person (in this instance a sibling) are getting played out in your current relationships?

2) How is the misdirected anger being maintained or kept alive?

There is also a relationship between anger and eating disorders, as pointed out by Dr. Judi Hollis in her book, *Fat Is a Family Affair*. Some survivors who participated in my research on sibling abuse reported that they were experiencing eating disorders, and were bulimic or anorexic. Hollis feels that people with eating disorders use food to push down the anger within them that they are attempting to deny. On the outside, the survivors might smile and seem not at all angry, but in reality they are seething with anger over their victimization by a sibling. A vicious recurring cycle develops in which the individual uses food to gain not only pleasure but solace from his or her turbulent feelings.

It makes sense that survivors' anger at their siblings (and in some instances their parents) affects the extent or frequency of their continuing contact with their families. Many of the survivors report very little interaction with their families, because of the abuse and the painful memories and accompanying feelings that interaction would provoke. Some survivors even report suffering panic attacks whenever they are in contact with family members:

A survivor writes:

There is still a lot of resentment toward my parents for being so irresponsible. I blame them for some of the confused feelings I have regarding sex. In fact, I blame them much more than I do my brothers because my brothers were just victims like myself.

Problems in Sexual Functioning

Survivors of sibling sexual abuse reported problems in sexual functioning resulting from their abuse. Two kinds of dysfunction were reported: avoiding all sexual contact, and being compulsively sexual.

Some female survivors reported that because of their sexual abuse by older brothers, they have an aversion to sex, even in marriage.

A study participant whose sexual abuse began at age eight and continued several times a week during her teenage years writes:

I've spent eight years in therapy for sexual abuse. I still freeze up when I'm touched in the vaginal area, which makes sex very unfulfilling and has been a big factor in the breakup of my relationships.

Another survivor shares her abuse-related feelings about sex:

I have been deeply affected by the sexual abuse from my brother. Even after years of therapy, it's hard for me to be truly open sexually with a man. I often experience shame and disgust around sex and tend to focus on the man's experience and pleasure rather than on my own. I have a hard time initiating sex. I often experience myself as a sexual object to be used and contemptuously discarded by men.

Childhood sexual abuse by a sibling has caused these survivors to fear and avoid marriage:

I am scared every man is going to make sexual advances toward me. I'm afraid of ever getting married because I'm afraid my husband might abuse me.

I feel uncomfortable with men. I do not trust them. I wonder if I will ever be able to be married to a man of excellent character and moral quality and have a healthy home life.

Other survivors reported an opposite reaction to their sexual abuse, that is, they were compulsively sexual: they were having repeated, frequent sex, sometimes with many different partners. This type of sex is not about joy and sharing, but simply expresses tension and fear. It might best be understood as the survivor's unconscious effort to overcome and deny the feelings of powerlessness, shame, and rage that resulted from being sexually exploited as a child. Sometimes survivors have compulsive sex because they feel so bad about themselves, that sex is the only way they know to try to feel better, to seem desirable to *someone*, anyone. That method of coping is an indication of low self-esteem, thinking that being used sexually is the only value you have.

Research indicates that a higher percentage of adults who were sexually abused as children have sexual problems than those who were not abused.[9] Other studies indicate that an unusually high percentage of both male and female prostitutes report having been sexually abused as children.[10]

A Tennessee survivor writes:

> *I allowed others to take sexual advantage of me. I was sexually abused in my first marriage. I struggled for years with not knowing what normal healthy sexual experiences were.*

A Texas survivor describes her promiscuous behavior as an attempt to punish men for her abuse by her brother:

> *I became very sexually active after leaving home at twenty. I did not want to have meaningful or strong relationships with any one but to have sex with many men and never see them again, so that they might have a feeling of being used and hurt.*

Another survivor writes:

> *I was promiscuous as a college student. I had extreme difficulty telling a man what I needed in a relationship. I felt I had to give a good performance. I had absolutely no self-confidence. I equated sex with love.*

Addictions

Sibling abuse survivors reported that their abuse has affected their adult lives in the form of addictions, such as eating disorders, alcoholism, and drug abuse. A survivor who was the victim of sexual abuse from both her brother and her father associates her eating disorders with her abuse:

> *I have eating disorders. I am bulimic and at times anorexic. These have to do with the denial of needs and the shame and hate I have regarding taking things into my body.*

Other survivors reported having problems with drugs and alcohol. Research indicates that there is a high incidence of sexual abuse in the histories of female drug abusers.[11] Some studies have found as many as 30-44 percent of substance abusers report childhood sexual abuse.

This survivor was very forthcoming about having an alcohol abuse problem, but is getting help:

> *I still tend to blunt my feelings or drown them in booze. I am in Alcoholics Anonymous.*

Depression

Many sibling abuse survivors reported experiencing depression as adults, which they directly associate with the sibling abuse they suffered as children.

Asked how her sexual abuse by a sibling has affected her as an adult, a 42-year-old woman responded:

> *Terribly! I have seriously considered suicide. I experience severe depression requiring medication.*

Studies of the adult survivors of childhood sexual abuse (not necessarily by a sibling) report a high incidence of depression. For example, a study of 278 university women found that approximately 15 percent had experienced sexual abuse as a child, and that they in turn show greater symptoms of depression than those who were not abused.[12] It is probable that the depression stems from the sense of powerlessness the survivors felt at the time of their abuse, feelings they continue to experience in adulthood.

Many sibling abuse survivors continue to be haunted by the feeling that they can do nothing about what occurred, like the victims who told their parents but were not believed, or whose parents ignored the situation.

In the words of one such survivor:

> *If you can't trust and depend on your own family members, your siblings and parents, whom can you trust?*

Twenty-six percent of the participants in my research on sibling abuse reported that they had been hospitalized for depression, a significantly high rate. Based on these figures, it is reasonable to assume that even more survivors had sought help for their depression on an outpatient basis.

Depression affected some survivors so seriously that it led to suicide attempts. A full one-third, 33 percent, of the participants in my study reported having tried to kill themselves. Other studies involving sexual abuse victims report even higher suicide attempt rates.[13]

Anger and depression are viewed as two sides of the same coin. Often, depression is regarded as anger that individuals turn in on themselves instead of expressing it at its legitimate object. The depression felt by sibling abuse survivors probably results from the anger they actually feel toward their perpetrators, but they have redirected toward themselves. This self-directed anger is especially likely in the case of survivors who blamed themselves for their abuse in the first place and whose parents ignored their pleas for help, reinforcing the conclusion that somehow they deserved to be abused.

Post-Traumatic Stress Disorder

People who have been severely traumatized often react with a collection of symptoms that have been identified as Post-Traumatic Stress Disorder (PTSD). Various types of trauma may evoke this reaction, including serious threats to one's life or integrity, threats or harm to one's family or friends, the sudden destruction of one's personal property or the community in which one resides, and witnessing someone seriously injured or killed as a result of physical violence or an accident. Mental health professionals are now adding to this list the trauma suffered by those who are sexually abused.

Some sexual abuse survivors deny or repress the memories of their victimization, and others attempt to blunt their painful feelings or memories through the use of alcohol or drugs. Despite this conscious or unconscious avoidance of their memories, in cases of Post-Traumatic Stress Disorder, the survivor might actually *reexperience* the abuse in any number of ways. The survivor might have flashbacks during the day or night or nighttime dreams in which the abuse is happening all over again. The flashbacks can consist of seeing the abuse happening, hearing sounds associated with the abuse, smelling odors (for example, if you were always abused on the day your mother baked fresh bread, the smell of fresh bread might bring back feelings from the abuse), or having emotions that are more intense than the current situation calls for, or that seem unconnected to what is currently going on. Sometimes being touched in a certain way or by a certain person will bring back the experience of abuse.

Sibling abuse survivors with PTSD often experience severe anxiety at family gatherings later in their lives, when they are once again in the presence of the siblings who perpetrated the abuse. In order to avoid these painful feelings, survivors with post-traumatic stress disorder often limit their contacts with other people, and they may withdraw altogether from interacting with family members, even when they don't have full memories of the abuse they suffered. They may only know how uncomfortable and tense they feel around family members or others who remind them of the person who abused them.

These reports come from sibling sexual abuse survivors who are suffering Post-Traumatic Stress Disorder:

> *Until recently sexual intercourse was not very enjoyable. Well, I would enjoy it, but I could never achieve an orgasm. Sometimes sex would become so emotionally upsetting that in the middle of it, I would remember the past, and the moment would be destroyed and I'd usually cry.*

> *Sometimes I will be thinking about what my brother did to me, and when my husband approaches me for sex, I will push him away. I find myself daydreaming about the whole nightmare of my sexual abuse. It's as if it's still happening and is never going to stop.*

> *I have a great deal of difficulty in my sexual relationship with my husband. Often I have had flashbacks during sex that are debilitating.*

Although some survivors reacted to their victimization with flashbacks and anxiety, others with PTSD showed a complete absence of the normal emotions that one might expect them to feel. This effect is referred to as psychic numbing, or emotional anesthesia. Those who react in this manner feel detached or estranged from other persons, and lose the ability to enjoy previously enjoyable activities. The numbness is likely to be most pronounced in close relationships with other persons.

Summary

In this chapter, you have read accounts by sibling abuse survivors that illustrate how the childhood abuse they experienced from their siblings has influenced their adult lives. I hope that while you read these accounts, and as you complete the task that follows, you can look at your own current life and determine whether any problems-in-living that you are experiencing are related to the abuse you suffered from a sibling.

A Task for You

This task will help you explore the impact of victimization by a sibling on your present-day life. In your notebook, make a list of the 10 ways you've read about in this chapter that sibling abuse survivors have been affected by their childhood experience:

1) Poor self-esteem
2) Problems in relationships with the opposite sex
3) Difficulty with interpersonal relationships
4) Repeating a victim role in other relationships
5) Continued self-blame
6) Anger toward my abuser
7) Problems in sexual functioning
8) Addictions (eating disorders, alcoholism, drug abuse)
9) Depression
10) Post-traumatic stress disorder

Using the scale illustrated, write down a number for each item on the list that indicates how much you have been affected by your abuse experiences.

1	2	3	4	5
not at all		somewhat		very much

We refer to problems occurring in every day life as "problems-in-living." The sibling abuse survivors in the survey identified these ten categories as effects they experienced in reaction to their abuse by a sibling. But you may have other problems-in-living from your childhood abuse that we haven't discussed. Think about your life and the problems you find yourself thinking about, discussing with friends, or for which you might even have sought professional help. Also, are there any chronic physical problems that you might attribute to the stress you continue to experience from the abuse you suffered? In your notebook, identify any other effects you think might result from your abuse by a sibling.

Endnotes

8 H. Lerner, *The Dance of Anger.* (New York: Harper & Row, 1985) p. 10.

9 J. Briere, "The effects of childhood sexual abuse on later psychological functioning: Defining a post-sexual abuse syndrome." Paper presented at the Third National Conference on Sexual Victimization of Children, Children's Hospital National Medical Center, Washington, D.C. (April, 1984). K. Meiselman, *Incest: A Psychological Study of Causes and Effects with Treatment Recommendations.* San Francisco: Jossey-Bass, 1978).

10 E. S. Blume, "The walking wounded: Post-incest syndrome," *SIECUS Report XI* 1 (September 1986), pp. 5-7. M. Janus, "On early sexual victimization and adolescent male prostitution," *SIECUS Report XII* 1 (September 1984), pp. 8-9. M. Silbert & A. Pines, "Early sexual exploitation as an influence in prostitution," *Social Work* 2 (1983): pp. 285-289.

11 J. Benward & J. Densen-Gerber, "Incest as a causative factor in antisocial behavior: An explanatory study," *Contemporary Drug Problems* 4 (1975): 323-340.

12 J. Briere & M. Runtz, "Symptomatology associated with prior sexual abuse in a non-clinical sample," *Child Abuse and Neglect* 12 (1988): 51-59.

13 M. DeYoung, *The Sexual Victimization of Children* (Jefferson, NC: McFarland, 1982). J. Briere, D. Evans, M. Runtz, & T. Wall, "Symptomatology in men who were molested as children: A comparison study," *American Journal of Orthopsychiatry*, 58 (1988): 457-461.

"My life was a mess from the abuse I experienced from my siblings until I sought help from our community mental health center. Gradually, I am getting my life turned around."

Chapter 9

Now What? Life Choices for Sibling Abuse Survivors

You have now read the experiences of many adults who were physically, emotionally, or sexually abused by their siblings during their childhoods. As you read these painful and sometimes tragic accounts, you have had the opportunity to reflect on your own experiences and decide whether they were actually abuse, rather than sibling rivalry. The tasks you completed at the end of each chapter have helped you in rethinking the treatment you experienced from a sibling and identifying what was abusive. If you were physically, emotionally, or sexually abused and you've read this far, one question still remains: "Now what? Now I know I *was* abused by my sibling. Now what do I do about it?"

Options

Acknowledging and understanding the abuse.

Although you might have experienced abuse from a sibling, the emotional climate in your home may have let you feel confident that you were loved. Or perhaps your parents became aware of the abuse shortly after it began, and intervened to put a stop to it. Although you were able to identify ways you were abused in earlier chapters of this book, you may not necessarily relate the abuse to any significant problems-in-living you have now as an adult.

If this is so, you are indeed fortunate. Remember that the purpose of this book is not to talk you into becoming a victim, but to help you determine whether you were abused by a sibling, and understand how the abuse might have affected your life as an adult, and to encourage you to start on the path to healing.

For those of you who are fortunate enough not to have experienced any effects in your adult lives from your abuse by a sibling, your response to the question, "Now what?" might consist of being aware of your sibling's treatment of you, being alert to whether or not the abuse is still occurring, either overtly or covertly, in your present adult life, and, if it is, dealing with the sibling who is still hurting you. If you are a parent, your response to the question may also include a decision to be more aware of what is happening between your own children.

Confronting the abusive sibling.

Reading this book and completing the tasks at the end of each chapter might have made you realize how angry you are at the sibling who abused you. Your first reaction to this anger might be an urge to confront that sibling over what he or she did to you.

Sibling abuse survivors must be cautious in deciding whether to follow through on any confrontive urge. Many sibling abuse survivors have reported that, when they confronted their abusive sibling(s), they were revictimized in the interaction.

These two survivors describe what happened to them:

Recently after hearing about rape victims who confront their rapists as part of their therapy, I decided on my own to confront my brother who sexually molested me as a child. He blamed all of it on me. He said I led him on, that I could have stopped it, or I could have walked away if I had wanted to. He made it out to be all my fault! He wouldn't apologize. I went away more angry than ever and now I don't know what to do with my anger. I don't care if I ever see him again.

Recently when my brother and I were together, we started talking about our lives when we were kids. I told my brother how hurt I was about the names he called me when I was little. I was always the butt of my brother and an older sister's jokes. (I was a gawky, unattractive kid when I was little.) I thought my brother might at least say he was sorry but he laughed it off. Later, he told my parents what I had said and they brushed it off saying, "That was twenty years ago!" They couldn't even begin to understand how I felt. I knew then and there it was useless to talk to them about this. They don't know that I have begun seeking counseling for the terrible feelings I have about myself that I think stems in part from the emotional abuse I experienced from my siblings (and my parents).

These responses are not unusual—not helpful, not responsible, but also not unusual. In their confrontations, the two survivors did not suddenly spew out their anger and pain, hitting the perpetrators between the eyes, so to speak, with what happened. Instead, they discussed in a calm, deliberate, and mature manner what their sibling perpetrators did to them when they were children. There's a good reason for using this approach: psychologists say that whenever people feel they are under attack, they set up mental and emotional defenses. These defensive measures include denying what occurred, offering excuses or rationalizations, and projecting the blame onto someone else, often the victim. Taking responsibility for one's behavior, acknowledging what one has done, and asking how to make amends are the unfortunately rare actions of mature, responsible adults. We can see all too many clear examples of defensive responses by public figures from politicians to corporate tycoons who have been caught engaging in unscrupulous behavior. When perpetrators of abuse become defensive about their behavior, they are following a social trend.

So if your response to the question, "Now what?" is to want to immediately confront your sibling about the abuse inflicted on you as a child, take a few minutes to seriously think about this. Ask yourself: "Why do I want to do this? Is it for revenge, to vent my anger, to extract an apology, or just to get my perpetrator to acknowledge what he or she did?" Ask yourself whether your goals are realistic.

Confrontations are not necessarily recommended. You can heal without directly confronting the perpetrator, because the healing is about what happens inside *you*, not about how anyone else behaves or reacts.

Think about your perpetrator. How does he or she behave in stressful situations? Recognize that any confrontation is likely to create lots of stress for both of you. Can you sit down with this person and calmly discuss such an emotionally charged issue as the abuse you suffered from him or her? How might your sibling react—by going into a rage, denying what happened, projecting the blame back on you, or threatening you? *Or* by accepting the responsiblity and asking for your forgiveness?

Take some time—at least a few weeks—to think about confronting your sibling. If you still want to go ahead after asking yourself these questions, then carefully structure—in advance—what you are going to do and how you are going to do it. Here are some of the many questions you will need to think about:

1) How are you going to approach your sibling? Will you write or telephone? Will you simply suggest that you want to meet to talk about something that concerns you, or are you going to share the purpose of your meeting beforehand?

2) Where should you and your sibling meet? Will you suggest that it be at one or the other's home, or on neutral ground, such as a restaurant or the park? What are the risks involved in meeting at whatever place you choose? For example, if one or both of you becomes very upset—cries, becomes angry, begins shouting, threatens—what will you do?

3) Will you meet your sibling perpetrator alone or have someone with you? What are the risks involved in meeting alone? What might happen if you ask someone to come with you—your spouse, a friend, an attorney, a professional mediator? What if your sibling unexpectedly brings someone to the meeting?

4) What are you going to say? How are you going to say it? Will you be able to convey what you want to express? Will your feelings of anger and hurt help or hinder you?

5) How might your sibling respond to your confrontation? Will he or she be angry, deny it ever happened, blame you, threaten you in some way? What if your sibling suddenly gets up and leaves?

6) How will you respond to your sibling's reaction to what you will be saying? What if your sibling denies what you are saying, becomes very angry, projects the blame on you, how will you respond? Will you become defensive, push the issue further, threaten to involve other family members in order to reinforce your case, or simply let it go?

7) What are the possible outcomes of such a confrontation? If your sibling acknowledges what happened and apologizes or asks for your forgiveness, will your relationship improve? If your sibling does not take responsibility for his or her behavior, what will the cost be to your relationship with this sibling, with other siblings, or with your parents?

The decision to confront your sibling about the abuse he or she inflicted on you when you were children is so critical, and its possible consequences so serious, that you must carefully anticipate every step of this action. Before you approach your sibling, talk to a professional counselor about what you intend to do. If you act impulsively, you may be victimized again by your sibling's defensive response. Before any confrontation—or even instead of one—

direct the energy you would spend on the confrontation toward your own healing by getting the help of a therapy professional (more on therapy later in this chapter). Remember, there is only one person whose behavior you can change—**YOURSELF**.

Ignoring the abuse.

Another option is simply to ignore the abuse. Its effects—your anger, distrust, and perhaps other problems-in-living—might weigh heavily on you at times, but your past reaction has probably been, "If I ignore it, eventually it will go away." And perhaps, even after reading this far, you see no reason to change. After all, the old adage says, "Time heals all wounds." Right?

Think again. The number of people who seek help from mental health professionals and join support groups for abuse survivors suggests how false this statement is. Time does *not* heal all wounds. Ignoring or trying to forget the abuse you experienced, either by acting as if it never happened or saying to yourself that eventually the pain will go away, simply does not work. It still affects you, perhaps in ways that are difficult to recognize or admit to yourself. It hasn't gone away, just underground, like a fire in a coal mine.

To use the analogy from the first chapter of this book, the abuse you experienced from a sibling can be like a heavy weight on you. The emotional pain the abuse created never seems to completely go away, but with professional help you can develop the psychic "muscles" to lift the weight and either bear it more easily or set it where it belongs—back onto the abuser.

Thus, if your first response to the question, "Now what?" was to reassure yourself that the painful memories stirred up by reading the earlier chapters will go away if you just ignore the feelings, I urge you to reconsider. The emotional pain you are experiencing may slip below the level of conscious awareness at times but, like an infection in your bloodstream, it will reappear. You must confront that pain and deal with it. Which leads us to the last option.

Seeking healing.

Seeking professional help for problems may seem like admitting that you have a weakness or a character flaw, or that you have accepted defeat. But stop to think how often you seek professional help in other areas of your life, without implying any weakness or flaw. For example, if you tried to start your car and found the engine was dead, you might check the battery and spark plug connections and the gas gauge, but would you undertake major repairs on the engine yourself? If you're not a trained mechanic, probably not. You'd probably admit your limitations in the area of car repair and seek the help of a professional—a mechanic. Likewise, when you're ill, you contact a physician. However, when it comes to problems-in-living, many people seem to feel that they can tackle any problem that life presents, all by themselves.

It's not a sign of weakness to seek professional help. Nor is it a sign that you are "crazy." Rather, it is just the opposite. It is a sign of strength. Seeking professional help shows that you are concerned about yourself, that you recognize that your life is not as you wish it to be, and that you want to make it better. Seeking professional help is an important step on the path of healing.

"But where do I go for professional help?" you ask. "I can't afford a high-priced psychiatrist, and anyway, I'm not comfortable going to a psychiatrist." You don't have to go to a psychiatrist. A licensed psychologist or a clinical social worker can help you. Start your search by looking in the Yellow Pages of your telephone directory, under the heading, "Marriage and Family Counselors." Social agencies and community mental health centers that offer counseling services, as well as therapists in private practice, will be listed here. Social agencies and community mental health centers generally do not charge as much for their services as private therapists, because these agencies are subsidized by the state or perhaps by United Way contributions. These agencies generally charge a sliding fee based on an individual's income. If you would rather see a private therapist, the cost of services may be covered by your health insurance.

If a listing in the Yellow Pages doesn't provide sufficient information about a private therapist's credentials, call and ask. If your state requires counselors to be licensed, ask whether the therapist is licensed. Ask if a therapist is a member of a professional association such as the American Association of Marriage and Family Therapists (AAMFT), the American Psychological Association (APA), or the National Association of Social Workers (NASW). If you are contacting a family counseling agency, you might wish to inquire whether the agency is a member of the Family Services Association of America (FSAA), an association whose member agencies are required to meet certain professional standards.

If the abuse you experienced from a sibling was sexual in nature, you might wish to contact your local rape crisis center to find out what counseling resources are available in your community. Although these agencies use the word "rape" in their name, their services usually address the needs of a wide range of sexual abuse victims, including adults who were sexually victimized as children. Frequently, these agencies sponsor support groups for adult survivors of childhood sexual abuse. These groups are usually led by professionals, and can really help you heal.

As you begin your path of healing, be open about yourself with your therapist. If you don't feel that the therapist is helping you, discuss these feelings with the therapist. Clarify your expectations of the therapist and allow the therapist to do the same with you. You should feel comfortable with your therapist. If you're uncomfortable, you might try a different therapist, after discussing your feelings and concerns with your current therapist.

As in any profession, unfortunately there are a few unethical or incompetent therapists. If any therapist suggests that you work on sexual issues by being sexual with him or her, report that therapist to the state licensing authority as soon as possible, and find another therapist.

You won't regret seeking professional help. Simply by taking the first step and contacting a counselor in order to discuss the abuse you suffered as a child and the impact of this abuse on your life, you will begin to lift that heavy weight from your shoulders. Therapy is hard work. There is no one harder to deal with than yourself, as you know if you've ever tried to break a bad habit or follow a diet. But it can be done! And when you succeed, the success is worth every ounce of effort.

Are you willing to take another step on your path to healing? If so, seek professional counseling.

A Task for You

In this chapter, several options have been suggested that are available to you now as you think about the abuse you experienced. These options, and questions relating to each one, are listed below. Think carefully about the options and the consequences of selecting each of them. In your notebook, write the answers to the questions as you think about each option and its consequences.

Options:

Acknowledging and understanding the abuse.

1) Am I experiencing effects now as an adult from the abuse by a sibling when I was a child? If yes, what are these effects or problems-in-living? Compare your responses to the ten effects of abuse found on page 106.

   If you have not already done so, seeking professional help for these effects of your abuse or problems-in-living is important. You may wish to reread the final section of this chapter, on how to seek professional help, and complete the last task below.

2) Am I still being abused by my sibling(s) even though we are now adults?

   If yes, in what ways does this abuse still occur?

If you are still experiencing sibling abuse as an adult, such as being called a nickname you do not like, you might wish to talk to your siblings about this and ask that they call you by your given name. If your current sibling abuse is more serious, you might wish to confront your sibling(s) about this or seek professional help. Please consider carefully your answers to the questions that follow, regarding confronting a sibling or seeking professional help.

Confronting my sibling.

Because confronting your sibling abuser is such a serious step with potentially harmful results, the questions that were presented in this chapter are repeated below in order to give you an opportunity to write out an answer to each one and review your responses in the coming weeks before you decide to set up a confrontation.

1) Picture your sibling abuser in your mind now as an adult and write a description of his or her personality. Looking at a photograph of your sibling as an adult may help you.

2) How will you approach your sibling about the abuse you experienced?. Describe what you will do—write a letter, call on the telephone, or make contact in some other way?

3) Where will you and your sibling meet to discuss your abuse?

4) What risks are involved for you in meeting there? For example, what will happen if you start to cry, or if your sibling becomes angry and starts shouting?

5) Will you meet with your sibling alone? If you bring someone with you, who will that be? How will that person behave if, for example, you begin crying or your sibling becomes angry? Whom might your sibling bring to the meeting?

6) Specifically, what are you going to say? Write out the conversation indicating what you intend to say, what you think your sibling's response will be, your comment in response, etc. Consider several possible responses that would be in character for your sibling, based on what you know of him or her. As in a play script, include in the dialogue the emotional energy that might be part of the words, for example, "[*angrily*] I never did any such thing!"

7) Just as there are three primary colors (red, green, yellow), that when blended create all the other colors, so some psychologists say that there are four primary emotions we experience as human beings, that are the basis of all other emotions. Write down these four feelings and *circle* the one or two primary feelings you think *your sibling* will display during your confrontation with him or her.

   sad *glad* *mad* *scared*

   Now put *brackets* around the one or two primary feelings you think *you* will experience in your confrontation with your sibling.

8) Write down in your notebook at least two possible outcomes (positive or negative) that you think will result from your confrontation with your sibling.

Ignoring the abuse.

Refer again to the task you completed on page 106, where you put a number from one to five on how seriously you've been affected by the abuse you experienced. Analyze your responses to those questions.

How many questions have you answered 5?

How many rated a 4?

Are there more 4s and 5s than 3s, 2s or 1s?

How many years ago did your abuse by a sibling occur?

Has ignoring the abuse these many years removed any of these effects: *poor self-esteem; problems in relationships with the opposite sex; difficulty with interpersonal relationships; repeating a victim role in other relationships; continued self-blame; anger toward your abuser; problems in sexual functioning; addictions (eating disorders, alcoholism, drug abuse); depression; post-traumatic stress disorder?*

If your answer is "no," please continue by answering the final section.

Seeking healing.

The fastest, most effective way to achieve healing is to get professional help in dealing with the effects of the abuse you suffered from a sibling as a child. It will take work and it doesn't happen automatically, but the reward of reclaiming your own life is worth the effort.

1) In your notebook write down the feelings from the list below that illustrate your own emotions when you think about seeking professional help:

scared	*worried*	*hopeful*	*anxious*
glad	*embarrassed*	*reluctant*	*fearful*
confident	*pleased*		

2) As you read these paragraphs that recap the main ideas from this chapter, write down in your notebook any statements that are particularly meaningful to you.

Seeking professional help for problems-in-living may seem like admitting a weakness or character flaw, or acknowledging defeat. But stop to think how often you seek professional help in other areas of your life, such as calling for a mechanic when your car won't start, or a physician when you feel ill. Why is it that when we have problems-in-living, we think we should be able to handle them ourselves?

It is not a sign of weakness to seek professional help. Nor is it a sign that you are "crazy." Rather, it is a sign of strength and sanity. Seeking professional help shows that you are concerned about yourself, that you recognize that your life is not as you wish it to be, and that you want to do something about it. Seeking professional help is an important step on the path of healing.

Seeking professional help may seem scary. Any new experience brings with it feelings of anxiety and fear. However, you will find that your counselor will put you at ease, and will help you talk about yourself and the abuse you experienced. In the end, you will be glad you sought professional help.

3) Where can you go for counseling? Look in the listings of counseling agencies or private therapists in the Yellow Pages of your telephone directory, under the heading, "Marriage and Family Counselor." Write down in your notebook three agencies or private therapists whose offices you can get to by car or public transportation and their phone numbers.

   Remember, if you have been sexually abused by a sibling, your local Rape Crisis Center (look in the phone book under "Rape") may work with adult survivors of sexual abuse, or at least they'll be able to refer you to someone who does such work.

4) In your notebook, write what you might say in your first telephone call with the agency or therapist. Here's an example of how you might begin:

   "Hello, I'm calling to ask if you work with abuse survivors. Over the past months, I've become aware that I was abused by my sibling when I was a child and the effects this seems to have on my life, and I would like to talk to a therapist about it."

   Remember, it is fine to ask how much the counseling will cost and whether the fees are covered by your insurance. Also ask about the therapist's degree and whether he or she is licensed. In your notebook make a list of the questions you want to ask.

5) When you begin meeting with the therapist, what issues do you want to discuss *in addition* to the effects of the abuse on your life? Make a list—for example, destructive patterns of behavior, negative thoughts about yourself as a person (such as "I may be stupid in bringing this up, but ..."), hurtful or psychologically damaging behaviors with your own children that may stem from your experience of abuse, limited contact with family members, possible sibling abuse among your own children, etc.

Reminders

I **hope that as you read** these final words you are either on your way to seeking professional help for the abuse you suffered as a child at the hands of a sibling, *or*, happily, you have discovered that although you have some unpleasant memories and perhaps didn't get along well with your siblings, you were not physically, emotionally or sexually abused. Here are a few reminders about what you have read throughout this book and at the end of this chapter.

Sibling abuse is real! Physical, emotional, or sexual abuse by a sibling can have a serious impact on the victim, not only at the time it occurs but also for the rest of the victim's life. However, when you act in your own behalf by getting help for yourself, sibling abuse does *not* need to be a life sentence to anger, pain, isolation, or whatever you might be experiencing as effects of the abuse.

Help is available for dealing with these issues! You will not regret seeking professional help. Talking to a professional about the abuse you experienced and its impact on your life will be like having a heavy weight lifted from you.

Therapy is hard work. There is no one harder to deal with than yourself. But it can be done! And when you succeed, the success is worth every ounce of effort.

Best wishes on your journey of healing!

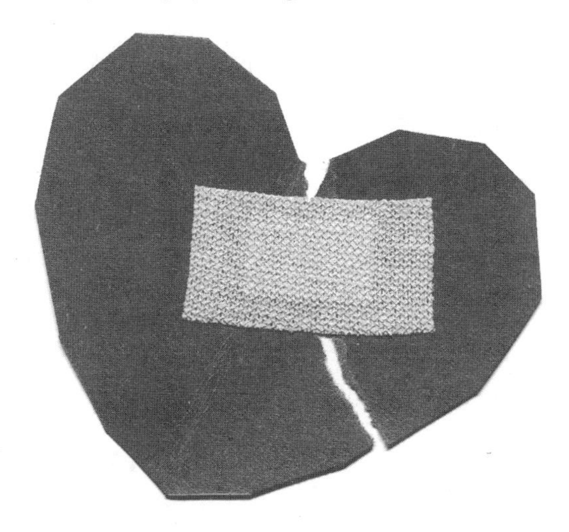

Recommended Books & Videos

The following is a list of books and educational and training videos that may be useful in dealing with sibling abuse, especially sexual abuse. Some may be helpful for the sibling who abused you, if he or she wants help. Each book or video has been reviewed by one or more staff or associates at the Safer Society. Several other useful books will be found on the Safer Society Publications list.

Boundaries: Where You End and I Begin.

Katherine, A. 1991.

A good, simply-written book on boundaries for everyone, it includes sexual abuse case examples along with several other issues.

Hazelden Publishing, 15251 Pleasant Valley Road, Center City, MN 55012-0176. 1-800-221- 6364.

For Guys my Age: A Book About Sexual Abuse For Young Men.

Taylor, M. 1990.

Hawthorn Center, 1847 Haggerty Road, Northville, MI. 48167. (313) 349-3000 ext. 584. Free.

Macho: Is That What I Really Want?

Bateman, P. & Mahoney, B. 1986.

Youth Education Systems, Box 223, Scarborough, NY 10510.

Men Surviving Incest.

Thomas, T.; Rockville, MD: Launch Press.

Secret Feelings and Thoughts.

Narimanian, R. 1990.

Philly Kids Play It Safe, 1600 Arch Street, New York, NY 10022.

Videos

Why God Why Me (1988). 24 minutes.

A tribute to the power of the human spirit; a true life account of a single woman's sexual abuse and her healing process.

Varied Directions; 69 Elm Street; Camden, ME 04843. (207) 236-8506.

Four Men Speak Out (1991). 28 minutes.

Four male survivors discuss how abuse affected their lives and the steps they are taking toward recovery.

Varied Directions; 69 Elm Street; Camden, ME 04843. (207) 236-8506.

Child Sexual Abuse: Both Sides Of The Coin (1991). 47 minutes.

A powerful video profiling the lives of two men who were abused. One becomes a sex offender, the other works through his rage.

Distributed by: Varied Directions; 69 Elm Street; Camden, ME 04843. (207) 236-8506.

Stories No One Wants To Hear (1993).

Survivors of sexual abuse by women speak about their experiences.

Varied Directions; 69 Elm Street; Camden, ME 04843.
(207) 236-8506.

To A Safer Place.

In this 58-minute ground-breaking video documentary, incest survivor Shirley Turcotte traces her abuse history within her family, dispelling myths while addressing the issues about incest.

AIMS Media; 9710 DeSoto Ave.; Chatsworth, CA 91311-4409.
(800) 367-2467.

No More Secrets: The Effects Of Childhood Sexual Abuse On Adult Survivors (1990).

Abused Survivors Know, Inc.; PO Box 323; Vienna, VA 22183.
(703) 281- 7468.

Once Can Hurt A Lifetime: Marilyn Van Derbur (1994).

30 minutes. *An educational video on the impact of acquaintance and date rape.*

One Voice; 1858 Park Road NW, Washington, DC 20010.
(202) 667-1160.

Surviving Rape: A Journey Through Grief.

Using interviews with rape victims, this 32 minute video reviews the five stages of grief that usually occur as a result of being raped: denial, anger, depression, bargaining, and acceptance.

AIMS Media; 9710 DeSoto Ave.; Chatsworth, CA 91311-4409.
(800) 367-2467.

Big Boys Don't Cry (1991).
50 minutes.

A documentary on the sexual abuse of males.

KGW-TV; 1501 SW Jefferson; Portland, Oregon 97201-2566.
(503) 226-5076 or (503) 226-5000.

A Theft Of Innocence (1989).
50 minutes.

A documentary on sexual abuse, victim impact, the sex offender, and recovery issues.

KATU-TV; Portland, Oregon.
(503) 231-4222.

Select Safer Society Publications

Adults Molested As Children: A Survivor's Manual for Women & Men by Euan Bear with Peter Dimock (1988; 4th printing). $12.95.

Family Fallout: A Handbook for Families of Sexual Abuse Survivors by Dorothy Beaulieu Landry (1991). $12.95.

Shining Through: Pulling It Together After Sexual Abuse by Mindy Loiselle & Leslie Bailey Wright (1994). $12.00.

Embodying Healing: Integrating Bodywork and Psychotherapy in Recovery from Childhood Sexual Abuse by Robert J. Timms, PhD & Patrick Connors, CMT (1992). $15.00.

37 to One: Living as an Integrated Multiple by Phoenix J. (formerly Sandra) Hocking. Upbeat, down-to-earth look at life after integration. (1996). *[In press, call for price]*

Men & Anger: A Relapse Prevention Guide to Understanding and Managing Your Anger by Murray Cullen & Rob Freeman-Longo (1994). $15.00.

When Your Wife Says No: Forced Sex in Marriage by Fay Honey Knopp (1994). $7.00.

Who Am I & Why Am I in Treatment? A Guided Workbook for Clients in Evaluation and Beginning Treatment by Robert Freeman-Longo & Laren Bays (1988; 8th printing). Workbook for sexual abusers. $10.95.

Why Did I Do It Again? Understanding My Cycle of Problem Behaviors
by Laren Bays & Robert Freeman-Longo (1989; 5th printing).Second in the series of workbooks for sexual abusers. $10.95.

How Can I Stop? Breaking My Deviant Cycle by Laren Bays, Robert Freeman-Longo, & Diane Montgomery-Logan (1990; 4th printing). Third in the series of workbooks for sexual abusers. $10.95.

Empathy & Compassionate Action: Issues and Exercises by Robert Freeman-Longo, Laren Bays, and Euan Bear. Workbook for sexual abusers on developing empathy. $12.00.

Safer Society Videos

Offender-Victim Communication: A Face to Face Session (1995). 57 minutes. This video helps break down denial in sexual abusers, helps to teach empathy, and provides survivors with answers to some of the questions they most commonly ask. $125.

The Banner Project: Breaking the Silence of Sexual Abuse (1994). 45 minutes. An educational video about the Banner Project and incest; three survivors discuss their personal recovery from abuse by a father, a mother, and a brother with the Banner Project quilts as a backdrop. $40.

Order Form

Date: ____________________

☐ Please send a catalog.

Shipping Address:

Name and/or Agency

Address

City State Zip

Billing Address (if different from shipping address):

Address

City State Zip

Daytime Phone ( )

P.O. No.

Qty	Title	Unit Price	Total Cost
		Sub Total	
		VT residents add sales tax	
		Shipping	
		Total	

Add 8% to all orders for shipping & handling

Bulk order discounts available

Rush Orders - add $10.00

Make checks payable to: **Safer Society Press**

Phone Orders with Visa/MasterCard Accepted

US FUNDS ONLY. All prices subject to change without notice.

Mail to:

THE SaferSocietyPress
PO BOX 340 • BRANDON, VT 05733-0340
PHONE: (802) 247-3132

Wiehe, Vernon R.

The brother/sister hurt.

WITHDRAWN
Monroe Coll. Library

DATE			
06/19/14			
2/19/14			

WITHDRAWN
Monroe Coll. Library

BAKER & TAYLOR